ACADEMIC VOCABULARY
IN MIDDLE AND HIGH SCHOOL

SELECTED TITLES FROM THE AUTHORS

Fluency Instruction, Second Edition:
Research-Based Best Practices
Edited by Timothy Rasinski, Camille Blachowicz,
and Kristin Lems

Integrating Instruction: Literacy and Science
Judy McKee and Donna Ogle

Reading Comprehension, Second Edition:
Strategies for Independent Learners
Camille Blachowicz and Donna Ogle

Teaching Academic Vocabulary K–8:
Effective Practices across the Curriculum
Camille Blachowicz, Peter Fisher, Donna Ogle,
and Susan Watts Taffe

Academic Vocabulary in Middle and High School

Effective Practices across the Disciplines

Donna Ogle
Camille Blachowicz
Peter Fisher
Laura Lang

THE GUILFORD PRESS
New York   London

© 2016 The Guilford Press
A Division of Guilford Publications, Inc.
370 Seventh Avenue, Suite 1200, New York, NY 10001
www.guilford.com

Printed in the United States of America

This book is printed on acid-free paper.

Last digit is print number: 9   8   7   6   5   4   3   2

Library of Congress Cataloging-in-Publication Data

Names: Ogle, Donna, author.
Title: Academic vocabulary in middle and high school : effective practices
   across the disciplines / Donna Ogle, Camille Blachowicz, Peter Fisher,
   Laura Lang.
Description: New York : The Guilford Press, 2015. | Includes bibliographical
   references and index.
Identifiers: LCCN 2015024190| ISBN 9781462522583 (paperback : acid-free
   paper) | ISBN 9781462522590 (hardcover : acid-free paper)
Subjects: LCSH: Vocabulary—Study and teaching (Secondary) |
   Interdisciplinary approach in education. | BISAC: LANGUAGE ARTS &
   DISCIPLINES / Reading Skills. | EDUCATION / Teaching Methods &
Materials /
   Reading & Phonics. | EDUCATION / Secondary.
Classification: LCC LB1631 .O45 2015 | DDC 428.1/0712—dc23
LC record available at *http://lccn.loc.gov/2015024190*

To all the colleagues and family
who have stimulated and supported my interest
in language and learning,
especially Bud, KJ, Camille, Peter, and Laura
—D. O.

To Bette, Reno, Diane, Joe, Matt, Jim, Jake, and Jesse,
with thanks for all the talk (and arguments!)
around the dinner table
that fed my interest in vocabulary
—C. B.

To all past and current students
from whom I have learned so much
—P. F.

To my sons, Jacob and Brian—
watching you learn, play,
and wrestle with language every day
inspires me always
—L. L.

About the Authors

Donna Ogle, EdD, is Professor Emerita at the National College of Education of National Louis University, where she co-directs the Reading Leadership Institute. She serves as a consultant to arts integration projects funded by the Terra Foundation for American Art and is senior consultant to the STEP intermediate reading assessment development project at the University of Chicago Urban Education Institute. Dr. Ogle is past president of the International Reading Association (IRA; now the International Literacy Association), the Reading Hall of Fame, and the Illinois Reading Council. She has focused her career on literacy development that enhances students' thinking and learning across the content areas.

Camille Blachowicz, PhD, is Distinguished Research Professor Emerita at the National College of Education of National Louis University, where she co-directs The Reading Leadership Institute with Donna Ogle. She began her career as a classroom teacher and reading specialist and directed the clinical program for reading specialists at National Louis. Best known for her work in vocabulary, Dr. Blachowicz is coauthor of 11 books and more than 200 chapters, articles, and monographs. She has been recognized as an Outstanding Teacher Educator in Reading by the IRA and named to the Reading Hall of Fame.

Peter Fisher, PhD, is Professor of Education at the National College of Education of National Louis University, where he teaches graduate classes in literacy education. He has published numerous articles and chapters on vocabulary instruction and is coauthor of the books *Teaching Vocabulary in All Classrooms, Teaching Academic Vocabulary K–8: Effective Practices across the Curriculum,* and *The Complete Guide to Tutoring Struggling Readers: Mapping Interventions to Purpose and the CCSS.*

Laura Lang, PhD, is a Lecturer and Instructional Leadership Coach at the University of Wisconsin–Madison. She has 18 years of experience as a high school English teacher, reading specialist, and literacy/instructional coach in both urban and suburban settings. Dr. Lang is currently working with schools in Wisconsin as they integrate the AIW (Authentic Intellectual Work) instructional framework into their practice. She is President of the Madison Area Reading Council, a local affiliate of the Wisconsin State Reading Association.

Preface

In this age of the Common Core State Standards (CCSS), the focus of K–12 education is clearly on preparing students for the demands of college and careers. Central to that effort is the importance of helping students learn the large number of words that occur almost exclusively in academic settings and also of helping them develop independent word-learning strategies. In addition, students need to learn how to comprehend the varied academic discourses of the content areas in which those terms appear.

As Nagy and Townsend (2012) explain, "There is a growing awareness of the importance of academic vocabulary, and more generally, of academic language proficiency, for students' success in school. There is also a growing body of research on the nature of the demands that academic language places on readers and writers, and on interventions to help students meet these demands" (p. 91).

We agree with their observations. As educators with years of experience working with students in both public schools and university settings, we understand well how essential the development of rich and strong vocabularies is for students' success. Our research and collaborations with secondary teachers have helped us develop ways to infuse vocabulary study with content learning. We are pleased to be able to share what we have learned in this volume and hope to continue to learn from you, our readers and colleagues, as we guide students in this lifelong journey of language growth.

The first three chapters of the book lay the foundation for our deeper examination of ways to build academic vocabulary and academic language in major disciplines with a focus on English language arts, social sciences, math, and science. We think teachers of other content areas can use these examples and the instructional strategies we highlight in their own teaching. A key to successful academic vocabulary work is collaboration among faculty and departments, a theme that appears frequently throughout the book. The final chapter provides a guide to the increasingly rich array of both print and electronic resources available.

In Chapter 1 we establish why secondary teachers need to prioritize vocabulary instruction across the content areas; to do this, we discuss research with secondary and college students and the CCSS prioritization of vocabulary. We explore in some depth the multifaceted construct of academic vocabulary, clarify the various terms associated with it, and explain our orientation. The chapter addresses the challenges teachers face in accelerating students' vocabulary learning in schools and provides a set of teaching guidelines.

Chapter 2 explains how academic vocabulary is embedded in academic language and how that language may pose difficulties for students' comprehension. We examine the nature and purpose of academic language as students encounter it in their coursework. The chapter also enumerates ways teachers can promote students' understanding and use of academic language as they read, write, and use the language orally.

Chapter 3 provides a broad overview of vocabulary instruction and highlights some of the seminal research relevant to instructional practice. It introduces some basic theoretical issues important to teachers and outlines our perspective on comprehensive vocabulary instruction and the roles of teachers, parents, students, and administrators in word learning.

Chapter 4 looks specifically at academic vocabulary and language considerations important for English language arts teachers. We ground our suggestions in the responsibilities teachers have for teaching vocabulary needed for the SAT and ACT, as well as to meet the CCSS. We also highlight the special resources within the English language arts that can help students explore relationships between language and cultural identity and become sensitive to the evolving nature of our language.

Chapter 5 addresses the importance of focusing on academic vocabulary in history and social studies and provides suggestions for how teachers can assess the knowledge students bring with them and then develop deeper understanding of key terms. This chapter also includes a discussion of how teachers can collaborate across content areas so students develop a consistent approach to vocabulary development.

Mathematics and science are examined in Chapter 6, with many examples from secondary classrooms providing teachers clear ideas of how to develop academic vocabulary as students learn content. We explore specific characteristics of vocabulary in these fields, with attention to the complexity of terms, their specificity and semantic relatedness, and their association with visual representations.

Finally, Chapter 7 provides a compendium of resources for questions related to teaching academic vocabulary. Luckily, we are addressing vocabulary in a materials-rich era, with many excellent print and electronic resources for teachers and students. As part of the chapter, we provide guidance in exploring these resources along with an examination of the leadership roles needed for a strong and effective vocabulary curriculum.

Acknowledgments

Donna would like to thank all the teachers who have collaborated in developing a deeper understanding of how vocabulary instruction can be infused in teaching history. Especially helpful were two project teams. First were the Evanston High School teachers, and especially Chip Brady, who directed the Congressional American History Project, Creating a Community of Scholars. Second, nearly a decade of collaboration with the Chicago Public Schools middle-level literacy team, especially Amy Correa and the Striving Readers Project directed first by Kenya Sadler and then by Elizabeth Cardenas-Lopez, provided an incredibly rich context for learning, experimentation, and development of assessment and instructional activities.

Camille would like to acknowledge and thank our colleagues and students at National Louis University, especially Ann Bates, Char Cobb, Connie Obrochta, Ellen Fogelberg, Char Cieply, Jesse Orbea, Roberta Buhle, and Kristin Kaczmarek; the members of the Reading Leadership Institute and their district teachers and administrators; colleagues from the Suburban Council of the International Reading Association; as well as Jim Baumann, Patrick Manyak, Mike Graves and all the participants in the MCVIP project.

Peter would like to thank all the teachers who have invited him into their classrooms and talked to him about their instruction, especially Liz Gates, Wendy Mohrenweiser, Dan Mullens, and Robyn Ward and the math teachers at New Trier High School. He is also grateful to Naomi Hersheiser and the teachers at Prairie Crossing Charter School for sharing their time and commitment to environmental education.

Laura would like to thank all of the inspiring public school teachers and students in and around Madison, Wisconsin, who have welcomed her into their classrooms.

She is especially indebted to Mary Swenson, Jennifer Breezee, and Lindsay Simonson, whose innovative approaches to vocabulary instruction are featured in the English language arts chapter. In addition, Laura would like to recognize her former colleagues, administrators, and students at New Trier High School, especially the members of the inaugural Northfield Literacy Team. A special thanks goes to her formal principal, Jan Borja, who encouraged her to "dream big," and to Donna, Camille, and Peter, who first introduced her to the complexities of literacy instruction many years ago.

We all are deeply grateful to Craig Thomas of The Guilford Press for encouraging our planning, nurturing our collaborations, and guiding us in shaping this book. The production guidance from Mary Beth Anderson was invaluable. This final text speaks to the expert team at Guilford who have shepherded the book to production. To all of them we express our gratitude.

Contents

CHAPTER 1

Vocabulary as a Key to College and Career Readiness

Succeeding in school, and in life beyond school, requires that students develop rich and precise vocabularies. We recognize this as true when, as adults, we are judged by the "quality" of our conversational vocabulary. Developing strong vocabulary knowledge is even more important for success in disciplinary learning. As Phythian-Sence and Wagner (2007) explain, "Acquiring the vocabulary we use for thinking and communicating is a linguistic achievement of nearly incomprehensible importance and complexity." Learning the content of disciplines such as science, mathematics, history/social studies, literature, and the humanities affords students new opportunities and challenges with language as they learn.

A significant challenge is that many of the terms students encounter are ones they have never heard spoken, and the concepts are often new and complex. In general, these terms are what we refer to as *academic vocabulary*. In some cases, students encounter these terms in several of the classes they take—terms like *analyze, representation, boundary*, and *resources*. Many other terms are only encountered when students read or discuss particular content; these are referred to as *domain-specific vocabulary*. Both of these types of vocabulary are developed best when teachers draw attention to them directly, guiding students in identifying and learning these words and phrases. As Nagy and Townsend (2012) explain in their article "Words as Tools: Learning Academic Vocabulary as Language Acquisition," "We use the metaphor of 'words as tools' to reflect our understanding that instruction in academic vocabulary must approach words as means for communicating and thinking about disciplinary content, and must therefore provide students with opportunities to use the instructed words for these purposes as they are learning them" (p. 91).

Vocabulary deserves our attention for many reasons besides those mentioned above. It is worth noting that the English language is distinguished from other languages by the total number of words it contains, and that this number is regularly expanding. According to estimates, the German language has a vocabulary of about 185,000 words, Russian has about 130,000, and French has fewer than 100,000. By comparison, English has well over half a million words. As Richard Lederer explained, "One reason English has accumulated such a vast word hoard is that it is the most hospitable and democratic language that has ever existed. English has never rejected a word because of its race, creed, or national origin. Having welcomed into its vocabulary words from a multitude of other languages and dialects, ancient and modern, far and near, English is unique in the number and variety of its borrowed words" (Lederer, 1991, p. 22).

Academic Vocabulary: A Challenge for Students

Students confront new academic vocabulary in each course they take; they must use these terms to identify, describe, and explain the key concepts and perspectives they encounter. Because each subject requires knowing a large number of content-carrying vocabulary terms, this is a significant challenge. Also, many terms students may understand in one context have specific and different meanings when encountered in different content areas. (For example, the term *representation* used in mathematics has quite a different meaning from the same term used in government or scientific contexts.) The large number and variety of academic terms within each discipline, and the range of academic terms students need to know across the courses they take, means that students must regularly attend to vocabulary and develop strategies for understanding and retaining the terms. In this process, many students become overwhelmed by the discipline-specific language—both the vocabulary and the more abstract and formal grammar through which ideas are communicated—and never acquire these tools that are essential to successful learning.

The Importance of Vocabulary for Comprehension

Vocabulary knowledge is a critical component of reading comprehension. According to Nagy and Scott (2000), 80% of comprehending informational text is tied to understanding the vocabulary. This close relationship between word knowledge and comprehension has been well established by researchers (Flood, Lapp, & Fisher, 2003; Graves, 2006; Pressley & Allington, 2014). In addition, researchers have also noted that the differences in students' vocabularies affect their achievement on standardized tests. Nagy and Herman (1984) reported that a 6,000 word gap separated students scoring at the 25th percentile from those at the 50th percentile from grades 4 to 12. The increasing numbers of English learners (ELs) in our schools also highlights the importance of giving specific attention to helping students expand their vocabularies for academic success.

It is no wonder that the Common Core State Standards for English Language Arts and Literacy in History/Social Studies, Science, and Technical Subjects (CCSS; National Governors Association [NGA] & Council of Chief State School Officers [CCSSO], 2010a) emphasize learning academic vocabulary. Students must know the specific terms used in the disciplines to understand the content they are learning. And part of the rationale for the CCSS emphasis is that there is a fairly large gap (almost a 2-year difference) between the level of vocabulary and reading required in high school subjects and what students encounter and need to use to succeed in college and the workplace.

The Teacher's Role and Responsibility

Many secondary teachers recognize the importance of helping students learn discipline-specific vocabulary and call attention to some of the terms they know students will need to use as part of their instruction. As Graves (2004) explains:

> Vocabulary instruction has always been an interest of middle and secondary school teachers, probably because they recognize its importance and are familiar with procedures for teaching vocabulary. For the most part, however, the vocabulary instruction that adolescents receive has been less comprehensive and less systematic than it could be, more often than not consisting solely of teaching the meanings of a small number of difficult words that come up in the selections students are reading. (p. 443)

Nagy and Townsend (2012) reinforce this perspective in their review of vocabulary research. They write, "Our review is shaped by our perceptions of the instructional context: K–12 vocabulary instruction in the United States seldom achieves the quality and intensity necessary to bring students not already familiar with academic language to the point of ownership of the instructed words" (p. 92).

Researchers who have studied effective vocabulary instruction often point to this lack of systematic instruction in academic vocabulary beyond the level of teaching a small set of individual words (Fisher & Frey, 2010; Gersten, Dimino, Jayanthi, Kim, & Santoro, 2010). While this basic approach to vocabulary instruction is important so that students acquire some of the key terms in each discipline they study, it is not adequate to support the large number of words they will encounter in their middle and high school courses. Too many concepts and words exist in most disciplinary courses for teachers to provide direct instruction of all the terms. What students require is better strategies for building their academic vocabularies so they can master the much larger number of words and phrases they will encounter and know how to use them appropriately in disciplinary contexts.

Students benefit from a more systematic approach to learning the vocabulary of their academic world. They need grounding in the ways that context functions to reveal the meaning of terms in specific situations in order to attend closely to the language they read and hear. In addition, students' vocabulary awareness increases substantially when they learn how to use morphology—identifying the key meaning-carrying parts of whole academic terms that are generally formed from Greek and Latin roots (Nagy & Townsend, 2012; Templeton, 2012). Most important, students need to have their interest in words and language nurtured by teachers and to be encouraged to hear and read from a wide variety of informative, well-written materials. Wide reading is one of the best ways for students to increase their vocabularies.

Research with college freshmen underscores the importance of helping students develop word-learning strategies. For example, Francis and Simpson (2003) conducted a study with two groups of college freshmen, one group scoring above grade level and the other group scoring below. Neither group was adequately prepared to learn vocabulary on their own; the students reported that the only way to learn new terms was by memorizing lists of words. Both groups scored poorly when asked to incorporate vocabulary meaningfully in their writing. Habits such as these do not serve students well. In recent decades, much of the text used in college and career settings has increased in complexity. College professors assign more readings from periodicals and primary sources than ever before (Milewski, Johnsen, Glazer, & Kubota, 2005) and often simply assume that students can comprehend them.

Students with a strong foundation in strategies for understanding and learning new and important terms will continue to expand their vocabularies; they will enjoy words and language more and feel confident in experimenting with language. Teachers play a critical role by establishing classrooms in which words are made interesting and language explorations occur regularly. Teachers also support vocabulary learning by reading aloud to students from a wide variety of informative, well-written materials. And because wide reading is one of the practices that most helps students to increase their vocabularies, providing interesting materials and giving students time to read is valuable.

It is also important that teachers draw on their students' linguistic reserves. Many of our immigrant students, especially those with Latin languages, need to be reminded to use their knowledge in their first languages and apply that knowledge to new terms in their second language. In some domains, nearly 70% of the academic terms have Latinate roots (Scott, Miller, & Finspach, 2012). Teachers who encourage students to compare and contrast ways of identifying and labeling ideas and concepts across languages instill curiosity in their students about how language functions in describing particular attributes and perspectives.

Perhaps understandably, most secondary teachers focus their attention on the content they teach more than on the tools and strategies they can teach to students to help them learn more efficiently and deeply. Interdisciplinary attention to learning strategies has not been strong in most middle and high schools. In this book we hope to bridge some of these divisions and provide a foundation for teachers to think and plan together for more consistent attention to vocabulary instruction. One theme we develop is the importance of teacher collaboration in creating an inviting context for language development and a consistent approach to vocabulary teaching and learning.

The Approach within the CCSS

The CCSS define literacy development as a shared responsibility of teachers across the content areas—not just in literature courses. The introduction to the CCSS makes this clear:

> The Standards insist that instruction in reading, writing, speaking, listening, and language be a shared responsibility within the school. . . . Part of the motivation behind the interdisciplinary approach to literacy promulgated by the Standards is extensive research establishing the need for college and career ready students to be proficient in reading complex informational text independently in a variety of content areas. (NGA & CCSSO, 2010a, p. 4)

The CCSS prioritize the reading and learning of content in history/social studies, science, and technical subjects in addition to traditional literature. The Anchor Standards for Vocabulary Acquisition and Use state that students should be able to do the following:

4. Determine or clarify the meaning of unknown and multiple-meaning words and phrases by using context clues, analyzing meaningful word parts, and consulting general and specialized reference materials, as appropriate.
5. Demonstrate understanding of figurative language, word relationships, and nuances in word meanings.
6. Acquire and use accurately a range of general academic and domain-specific words and phrases sufficient for reading, writing, speaking and listening at the college and career readiness level; demonstrate independence in gathering vocabulary knowledge when encountering an unknown term important to comprehension or expression. (NGA & CCSSO, 2010a, p. 25)

In addition, the content standards for grades 6–12 provide specific guidelines for the learning of disciplinary or domain-specific terms. Figure 1.1 shows the standards for grades 9 and 10.

Reading Standards for Literacy in Science and Technical Subjects

Standard 4: Determine the meaning of symbols, key terms, and other domain-specific words and phrases as they are used in a specific scientific or technical context relevant to *grades 9–10 texts and topics*. (CCSS.ELA-Literacy.RST.9–10.4)

Reading Standards for Literacy in History/Social Studies

Standard 4: Determine the meaning of words and phrases as they are used in a text, including vocabulary describing political, social, or economic aspects of history/social studies. (CCSS.ELA-Literacy.RH.9–10.4)

FIGURE 1.1. CCSS vocabulary-specific standards for literacy in science and history/social studies (grades 9 and 10).

Defining Academic Vocabulary

The more attention one pays to vocabulary, the more variety of terms one encounters. Readers of this book will want to distinguish between the specific uses of terms such as:

> *Content-area vocabulary*
> *Academic vocabulary*
> *Disciplinary vocabulary*
> *Domain-specific vocabulary*
> *General academic vocabulary*
> *Technical vocabulary*
> *Tier One, Tier Two, and Tier Three vocabulary*
> *Working vocabulary*

Academic vocabulary is fundamentally distinguished from conversational vocabulary as language that is not characteristic of informal and personal communication, but that reflects school-privileged knowledge. Academic vocabulary is learned through reading and writing and exploring new topics, often with a teacher's guidance. While identifying the vocabulary demands in content areas is important, we should also make a finer differentiation between general academic and domain-specific vocabulary, because the tasks involved in learning and using these terms are different.

General Academic Vocabulary

General academic terms are used across many contexts, and students are much more likely to encounter them as they read and listen. Because they are not used in everyday language, these terms deserve attention. When teachers focus on them, this pays off for students over the long term. Students will find these words in several content-area classrooms—especially in science and mathematics, but also in literature.

Domain-Specific Vocabulary

In contrast to general academic terms, domain-specific terms are found in much more limited contexts. They are also more likely to be highlighted and repeated frequently in content-area texts and resource materials. These are often the terms disciplinary teachers highlight and then require students to use in their speaking and writing. It is not uncommon for one chapter of a textbook or one section of a unit of study to include 20 to 30 new terms that students need to know and be able to use well. Textbooks often highlight these terms and include them in the glossary. However, when teachers use primary source material or collections of media or print articles, it is important that students receive guidance in knowing which terms are most central to the concepts for which they are being held accountable. Several vocabulary researchers and educators prefer to use the term *disciplinary vocabulary* or *technical vocabulary* for what the CCSS labels as domain specific. In this book we use these terms interchangeably.

Vocabulary Tiers

In distinguishing between general academic terms and domain-specific ones, the work of Isabel Beck and her colleagues (Beck, McKeown, & Kucan, 2013) is helpful. Beck and colleagues have differentiated vocabulary into three tiers, or groups. This framework is also used in Appendix A of the CCSS to explain the differences in general academic and domain-specific vocabulary.

Tier One Words

Tier One words are common, everyday words that most adults know and use regularly and that children develop in informal discourse. These words are useful but not conceptually hard to understand. ELs often develop mastery of Tier One vocabulary, and their oral communication abilities cause many teachers to overlook the need to focus more attention on the difficult academic vocabulary. These terms comprise most of our conversational vocabulary and language.

Tier Two Words

Tier Two words, also referred to as general academic vocabulary, include terms encountered in school learning across several topics and disciplines. These are words with real utility for students. Their meanings may vary by context—for example, the word *operation,* which has one meaning in mathematics, another in medicine, and yet another in work with machines. The root word *operate* also can take on varied meanings: operate the game board joystick or the motorbike, or to move strategically in social situations. These terms are not used generally in conversational English; they are more abstract and are more likely to pose challenges to students. Therefore, there is real benefit in teaching Tier Two words, so that students can become familiar with the terms and develop strategies that help them unlock meanings in a variety of contexts. Tier Two words are also important to highlight for ELs, so they don't overlook the specific and important meanings of these terms. As several educators have noted, lack of familiarity with the meanings of these terms as used on standardized tests has frequently caused ELs to respond inaccurately to items they actually know.

Tier Three Words

Tier Three words, in distinction from Tier Two words, are more specialized terms confined to particular academic domains or content topics. They are often the labels for key concepts being taught in a content area. These terms are often introduced and highlighted in the printed materials and textbooks students read. Teachers generally also introduce these terms as they are needed for specific content development. There are often many such terms, and it is the teacher's task to focus students' efforts on those that are most essential to the content being learned and with the highest overall utility for the students.

Benefits of Using the Three-Tier Framework

Teachers can use these three tiers of words to think about which words to teach. Tier One words are usually (but not always) learned through conversations with others at home and school, and do not require much direct teaching. Tier Two words are those that we consider *general academic terms* and that require attention by teachers. However, because they often are well known by adults, many teachers think that students understand these terms better than is often the case. These words thus deserve teachers' careful attention.

Tier Three words can be associated with the terms *domain-specific vocabulary, content-specific vocabulary* (Hiebert & Lubliner, 2008), or *technical vocabulary* (Fisher & Frey, 2008). In this book, we use the term *domain-specific vocabulary*; this use fits the distinction in the CCSS documents between academic and domain-specific vocabulary. The domain-specific words have less general applicability, but are often central to the concepts and ideas in content-area instruction.

Other Dimensions of Academic Vocabulary

Attention to academic vocabulary has led some researchers to further differentiate some categories of words that are helpful for teacher consideration. Both Hiebert and Lubliner (2008) and Baumann and Graves (2010) extract a set of words that are most useful in school tasks and in thinking about state and national standards. Hiebert and Lubliner call these *school terms*, and Baumann and Graves use the word *metalanguage* to identify this set of terms, which includes words like *genre, estimate, summarize, draft, compare and contrast,* and *punctuate.* These terms are particularly important for secondary students to develop, as they are used regularly on standardized tests and other performance tasks. Many students have fairly "fuzzy" ideas of what they may be asked to do on such tasks and do less well than they are able to, simply because they don't fully understand the tasks' demands.

It is worthwhile to mention "up front" the difference between how general academic vocabulary works in literature and how it works in other disciplines. In literature, Tier Two and Tier Three words (general academic terms and domain-specific terms) don't occur as major concept terms, but are likely to describe characters, settings, or aspects of conflict and style. Hiebert and Lubliner (2008) distinguish these terms because these are words authors of adolescent and young adult literature use in their work to "describe characters, their actions and settings in which the actions occur" (p. 111). These specific descriptive words (often adjectives and verbs) are often essential to understanding basic elements of literature, yet don't occur frequently within any one text. The challenge this poses to teachers of literary works is real; you will find much elaboration on how to address this challenge in Chapter 6, on teaching literature.

Identifying Important Academic Terms

Academic terms are identified and defined in various ways in textbooks and supplemental materials. Students need to learn how to use these different types of supports: italicized and boldface terms, footnotes or side notes, glossaries, lists of key terms with some activities to focus students' attention on the initial pages of each chapter, and so on. Some newer science programs include vocabulary cards with key academic terms and online games to help reinforce word learning. Reading and literature programs often focus on vocabulary to be learned, and some even teach students how to look at word families and make connections among terms. Teachers need to take advantage of these resources when they are available.

If you are not using a text-based or commercial approach to teaching, then some more general resources can help determine which words deserve focus. A useful, if somewhat dated, corpus of words was compiled by Marzano (2004) after the first round of state and content-area standards. Marzano analyzed the standards documents and compiled a list of academic terms that occur most frequently, orga-nized by grade bands and content areas. This resource is still useful to see whether widely used academic terms are being taught in your classroom and school.

Another useful list is one compiled by Coxhead (2000). Her Academic Word List was derived from her analysis of 3.5 million words used in texts across content areas. (One caveat is that these were college-level texts; another is that the texts were from England and New Zealand.) Words found in the first 2,000 most com-monly used terms in English were omitted, and then the terms that occurred at least 100 times were grouped into 570 word families (the stem, inflected forms, and forms with prefixes and suffixes). These words constitute about 10% of the words in content-area texts, so Coxhead's list remains a useful reference. The list has been used widely as a guide to academic vocabulary development and to determine the difficulty of materials. However, some vocabulary researchers have compared this list to terms in currently used textbooks and found little overlap. Therefore, it is important to use these lists as starting points, but to be most attentive to the con-cepts and terminology used in your own context.

In this book, we too provide several valuable tools you can use to determine which words are worth teaching at particular levels and in specific contents. Because there are varied criteria for what is important across the content areas, these issues are addressed in the specific content chapters.

Academic Vocabulary Is Embedded in Academic Language

Students may sometimes have difficulties with academic vocabulary, but they may also struggle to make sense of some of the language in which that vocabulary is embedded. The languages of home and school are different, and it is part of our job as teachers to introduce students to the academic discourses of the various dis-ciplines. They need to learn how scientists, mathematicians, historians, and so on write and speak about their subjects. Take, for example, this passage from a middle-grade science text:

> Although water ecosystems, like biomes, have dominant plants, they are most often identified as freshwater ecosystems or saltwater ecosystems. (Watkins & Leto, 1994, p. 63)

It is unlikely that you would come across a sentence structure like this any-where but in an academic discipline. If you were asked to identify the main idea, you might give it as follows: *Water ecosystems can be divided into freshwater and saltwater.* But notice how far apart the subject and object of this sentence are, and the information about *dominant plants* seems almost incidental. In Chapter 2, we look more closely at academic language structures and how best to address them. At this point, we simply want to draw your attention to the idea that students need to learn academic language in addition to academic vocabulary.

Elements of a Strong Vocabulary Program

Basic Components

Some basic components of a strong vocabulary program are applicable across most content areas. We share a few of these below, so that you can begin your engagement with this book knowing some of the foci that we elaborate more fully in later chapters.

First, it is important to analyze each vocabulary task both for the students and for the content you plan to teach. From the potential words, select those with the highest utility within the lesson or unit, and those that have generalizability across other units and other contexts.

Second, you will need to help students assess their levels of familiarity with the terms and help them attend to those that are most important, so that they can devote their energy to learning those that have been identified as central to the content. You can do this in various ways, including having students rate their knowledge of the terms; the goal is to draw students' attention to the most essential terms early in a lesson or unit of study, to help them focus cognitive resources where these will be most needed.

Third, you will need to use the opportunity at the initial stages of a unit to give students some instruction with the words. The nature of the activities will depend on what will benefit students most as they encounter the terms and discriminate their individual meanings. If there are many related terms, you might want to lead a lesson creating a semantic matrix highlighting specific attributes of each term. Or you might pair students and ask them to do a word search—locating the key terms in the textbook and then discussing the uses of each one. From this preview of the text, students could then construct working definitions of these words. This might also be a good time to do a lesson on morphology: Have students find words with the same root (e.g., *demo: democracy, democratic, undemocratic, demography*) and then decide on what the root (e.g., *demo*) means. Finally, students often benefit from a lesson on how to use context to build partial meanings of terms, and how to use the actual definitions texts provide.

Fourth, you will need to help students develop strategies for keeping these terms before them, for rehearsing them, and for deepening their understanding of their varied uses and meanings. Some academic terms also have more common meanings, and these different definitions need to be highlighted (e.g., see our *operation* example earlier in this chapter). Teachers should use these terms orally in useful contexts to give students access to both the written and oral forms of the terms.

The interplay between using academic terms orally and encountering them in print is another important aspect of academic vocabulary development. Students need several opportunities to use new terms orally, to build a familiarity with the terms, and to experiment with the contexts in which they are best expressed.

Additional Dimensions

Activities that help students construct fuller understandings of terms than simply learning their basic dictionary definitions are needed for the students to really know these terms. Definitions or descriptions, attributes, examples, ways to distinguish a term from similar ones, and nuances of when and how the terms are used are all important. When students have opportunities to explore varied uses of terms, to both see and hear these words used in several contexts, and to explore online resources for the terms, they become more aware of how "slippery" definitions are and how important context is to word use.

Many academic terms have their origins in Greek and Latin, so helping students attend to morphology and word histories will build their understanding. It is useful to help students connect several terms with a common root. As Nagy (1988) explains, vocabulary development depends on students' knowledge about these morphological families and on their ability to use this knowledge.

In some content-area materials, visual diagrams of concepts provide important information about the academic terms and need to be studied. Students should learn to match new concept terms with their visual representations, and to create diagrams or drawings if texts don't provide them.

Supporting ELs

ELs often are still developing their general, or Tier One, vocabularies while they are learning Tier Two and Tier Three vocabularies along with their English-dominant classmates. Because of this added learning challenge, it is helpful for teachers to provide sheltered English supports for them (Echevarria, Vogt, & Short, 2013). ELs who have Greek or a Latinate language as their first language have a special resource that can help them learn academic vocabulary. Many English academic terms (Tier Two and Tier Three words) have Tier One analogues in these languages. For example, words like *absurdo* (*absurd* in English), *mesa, arroyo,* and *pacifico* (*pacific* in English) are common terms in Spanish, but not in English. Such analogues make learning domain-specific words easier for EL students when teachers invite them to connect both languages and use their first-language resources.

The importance of encouraging students to think in both languages is supported in a recent research study by Scott et al. (2012), who found that in their identified academic terms for fourth- and fifth-grade science and math, about 70%

were Spanish–English cognates. With teacher encouragement, students can learn to draw on their first-language resources and find connections among vocabulary. Often what are more esoteric terms in English are more common forms in Spanish or French, as in the Spanish examples above. Simply asking students to make charts of the new words with the English and the home-language versions side by side can help both teachers and students find connections.

Laying the Foundation for Effective Teaching

Teachers who are serious about helping students expand their academic vocabularies also create classroom and school contexts where attention to words is a regular part of school life. Being serious about language development also means enriching students' background knowledge about vocabulary, making it personal, and connecting it to their lives beyond school. Three aspects of engaging, overarching language culture are described in this section.

Teachers' Modeling of Continued Language Development

Students need your help and encouragement in attending to and learning academic vocabulary. Teachers are role models and guides in helping students learn how to be "vocabulary smart." It is up to you to regularly note new and interesting words, as well as new uses of somewhat familiar terms, and to "think aloud" about these with students. For instance, bringing in a magazine article or a brochure and highlighting for students some unfamiliar terms as you read it orally to them can help students become more willing to do the same. As students move from middle to high school, some become hesitant to express their lack of familiarity with new words and concepts. Teachers can help students overcome this hesitation by bringing in words that are new to the teachers themselves, modeling how they noted the terms, and then showing students how they sought out the terms' meanings or engaging the class in trying to determine the meanings intended by the authors.

Teachers can also explain to students their own strategies for learning new words that are important. Some teachers may explain that they connect each new term to an already familiar word or experience, make a rhyme for the new word with something familiar, or connect the term to a person for whom it can be associated. Donna, one of our authors, often shares a true incident that occurred in the college dining room. A faculty member with whom she was eating paused as he looked up at a friend who walked into the room and exclaimed, "Wow, is she coruscating today!" Not knowing the word, I waited for a moment to ask what it meant. "Sparkling," he responded. And he was right—our colleague was bubbling and excited. This seemed like a lovely word to add to my vocabulary, but I was eating lunch and had no paper to write it down. I did try to make some associations so I could remember the word later: I thought, *coruscating*—sounds like a positive term, given how my friend used it, so *chorus* and then *gate* led me to think of a chorus line going through a stylized gate. Good thinking for the brief time I had before our conversation moved on to other topics. Later in the afternoon I knew I needed to write the word if I would be able to remember it; alas! Already I had confused my images—I saw Rockettes dancing—my visual imagery was strong, but the particular words were wrong. It wasn't until that weekend, when I read a book review that indicated "this made for coruscating reading," that I had found my word again. This time I wrote it on one of the 3″ × 5″ cards I often use for words I am trying to add to my vocabulary, and it stayed with me. Soon, I found the word in another context and added the sentence to my card (*The dew on the grass created coruscating lighting.*). Teachers who share experiences of their own efforts to learn words can open students to the realization that "adults" don't know all the words. Vocabulary expansion is a lifelong process.

For some teachers, holding on to a new word so it can be learned may involve creating a word card for the new term, putting the context in which it was encountered on the card, and then putting a description, definition, or illustration on the back side of the card. Some teachers like to keep a collection of words they are learning on their computers or smartphones. Showing students how terms are not just identified and defined, but also kept handy so they can be practiced, is a part of modeling how teachers as adults attend to new terms, develop understanding of their meaning, and then utilize strategies to retain them. Modeling how to practice and try out new words is important; many less-confident students think that "smart" people learn new words immediately when they see them or hear them. If students are going to get into the fun of building vocabulary, they need to know that it takes many exposures and attempts to use new terms. Some students may be surprised that teachers also need and use strategies to learn words; it makes word learning a genuinely shared adventure.

Teachers can also encourage students to take risks in the classroom by bringing in and sharing words they encounter in their own reading. This may involve taking time at the beginning of a class period to ask students to share any new terms they have recently found, and to explore the context in which the terms were used and what they may mean. Students can then use their own resource tools (hard copy or online dictionaries and glossaries) to develop definitions for the terms. A class bulletin board or website of new and interesting words keeps the importance of vocabulary growth fresh and personal for students.

Still another way teachers can model for students their own attention to vocabulary is to read books about words and language orally (Braun, 2010; McKeown & Beck, 2004; Neugebauer & Currie-Rubin, 2009). At every grade level, there are both fun and informative books that can nurture students' interests in language. Some introduce interesting names and words, such as *Crazy English* (Lederer, 1990) and *The Miracle of Language* (Lederer, 1991); some deal with the history of words and changing usages, such as *Thereby Hangs a Tale: Stories of Curious Word Origins* (Funk, 2007); some expand students' knowledge of specificity of usage, such as *The Professor and the Madman* (Winchester, 2005) and *The Real McCoy: Why We Say the Things We Say* (Hole, 2005); and some foster students' urge to create new words, such as *What's in the Word?* (Elster, 2005). Taking just a few minutes at the start or end of a class to read a short section about our language can sustain students' engagement with their own vocabulary development.

Nurturing Students' Interest in Words and Expanding Their Awareness of How Language Functions

Helping students become interested in words and language, and attentive to new words, phrases, and uses of language, is an essential foundation for vocabulary development. Students need to be interested in and knowledgeable about words and how they function as they encounter increasingly content-specific vocabulary. This involves teachers from all grades and disciplines. All teachers need to consciously check to be sure that they entice students with their own curiosity about words and help them explore unusual, new, and interesting uses of language. Although in later chapters we suggest many ways to do this, a good starting place is to check the collection of books in your classroom and tag those that deal with language and words.

Some teachers use magazines and contemporary culture to awaken older students to the creativity involved in creating new terms and revising uses of others. They involve students in thinking about vocabulary expansion by letting them find the most current words used for clothing, colors, hairstyles, sports, and music. Teachers often have middle-grade students write a glossary of terms for their favorite fantasy series. In these ways, teachers alert students to the reality that vocabulary is constantly growing and changing.

The joy of exploring books, magazines, and newspapers with interesting words and with information about language should be possible in all classrooms, at all levels. With all the online and graphic resources now available, it is quite easy to build a collection that will entice your students and open new worlds to them.

Making Vocabulary Learning a Shared Classroom and School Activity

Several schools we know have weekly words that the whole school population learns together. These are usually words that have general utility across subject areas, but they help reinforce and develop students' curiosity about words and the wealth of words in our language. Some schools put these words on the school marquee where all can see them; others send the words home so parents can post them on their refrigerators. Many schools have students describe these words and use them in the morning public address system announcements. Teachers who post the words on their classroom walls help students maintain their attention to expanding their vocabularies. These are just a few ways in which vocabulary can become visible in a school. In the following chapters, we share many ideas for making vocabulary exploration a lively part of classroom and school life. This is an essential starting place for all that we discuss as we focus on the central role of vocabulary learning. You may want to make a list of ideas that you have already implemented in your classroom and see how you can build on those, making them as effective as possible for all your students.

Concluding Thoughts

In this first chapter, we have set the context and furnished some common vocabulary for what follows in the rest of the book. As you read on, think about how you can support your students in expanding their general academic vocabularies— helping them attend to, explore, and use an increasing range of academic language in their oral and written discourse. By identifying general academic terms as well as domain-specific words needed for learning particular content, you can then decide which words to select for more focused instruction because of their importance and general utility for your students. We hope that this introduction has also helped stimulate your own thoughts about the vocabulary-learning opportunities you can provide in your classroom and throughout the school.

Students need regular opportunities to learn strategies for identifying and learning words they encounter as part of their academic work as they read and listen (receptive vocabularies); they also need support in being able to use those words as they speak and write about the content (expressive vocabularies). An added challenge in learning academic terms is that not only are there large numbers of new concept terms, but the way ideas are expressed varies by academic disciplines. So both the vocabulary and the forms of discourse are central aspects of language development.

CHAPTER 2

The Role of Academic Language in Disciplinary Learning

A middle school class was reading a chemistry text about microscopic organisms. It read:

> Algae represent a primary food source for various aquatic organisms. Photosynthesis by algae also contributes tremendously to the earth's supply of oxygen. (Watkins & Leto, 1994, p. 236)

The teacher asked the class what this meant, and one student suggested, "The organisms release oxygen into the atmosphere." Although there are several complex concepts in this paragraph (*primary food source, aquatic organisms, photosynthesis, contributes*), the misunderstanding seems to have occurred not because of the vocabulary, but because of the language structures. Normally one would expect the subject of the second sentence (*photosynthesis by algae*) to refer back to something in the first sentence—that is, to act as a cohesive device. However, in this case the previous topic is not expanded; instead, a new topic is introduced. The confusion could have resulted from the student's searching in the first sentence for something that adds to the supply of oxygen, and deciding on the last noun, *organisms*. The language of science, such as this, is an example of the academic language that students will engage with as they work their way through school. It is a language that they are unlikely to hear in any other context. In this chapter we explore the nature of academic language, as well as ways to familiarize students with such language.

What Is Academic Language?

When students come to school, they already know a variety of language registers—the different ways that they speak to adults, to each other, to a baby, or to clerks when shopping. Once in school, they are expected to use and understand school language, which is yet another register and a very different one. Cummins (2000) introduced terms to differentiate the types of language used in school and at home. He compared *cognitive academic language proficiency* (CALP), which is the ability to use and understand the academic language used for instruction, to *basic interpersonal communication skills* (BICS), which are the language skills a student might use on the playground or at home. In this categorization, in order to succeed in schools, our students need to learn CALP, which is cognitively demanding and academic, and which includes school-based discourse patterns. Often this academic language is characterized as *decontextualized*. Such language requires students to engage with ideas about people, objects, or events that are not present, and thus requires thinking beyond the immediate situation. Cummins's distinction was used primarily in relation to second-language learners, and is helpful as we think about the nature of academic language with all students. However, within the EL community there has been some debate about (1) whether academic language is truly decontextualized (Schleppegrell, 2004), and (2) which vocabulary and language patterns are academic and which are not (Aukerman, 2007). Coleman and Goldenberg (2010) suggest that the terms BICS and CALP have fallen out of favor because they imply a dichotomy that can be misleading. Although the general distinction is clear, the particular instances in which words and linguistic patterns are academic may be contextually defined by their use in the classroom. However, academic language is frequently regarded as the language used for instruction.

Other researchers and authors have attempted to come up with more detailed definitions of academic language. Some of them are displayed in Table 2.1. Although there are different emphases in these definitions, it is clear that they all refer to

TABLE 2.1. Definitions of Academic Language

Authors	Definitions
Bailey, Butler, LaFramenta, & Ong (2004)	The vocabulary, syntactic structures, and discourse features that are necessary for students to access and engage with their grade-level curriculum.
Chamot & O'Malley (1994)	The language that is used by teachers and students for the purpose of acquiring new knowledge and skills—imparting new information, describing abstract ideas, and developing students' conceptual understanding.
Scott, Nagy, & Flinspach (2008)	A register of English that has distinctive lexical, morphological, syntactic, and stylistic features.
Zwiers (2008)	The set of words, grammar, and organizational strategies used to describe complex ideas, higher-order thinking processes, and abstract concepts.

Note. From Blachowicz, Fisher, Ogle, and Watts Taffe (2013). Copyright 2013 by The Guilford Press. Reprinted by permission.

elements of language beyond the word level. So learning about academic language is more than learning academic vocabulary. It may also be more than being taught to be metacognitive. For example, Fang, Schleppegrell, and Cox (2006) argue:

> We have found that commonly taught cognitive and metacognitive strategies such as predicting, making connections, thinking aloud, inferencing, visualizing, summarizing, and dramatizing . . . are, although important, often inadequate to ensure text comprehension. We believe that children need additional strategies that can help them engage with texts with greater ease and critical mindedness. (p. 248)

In addition to being metacognitive about comprehension and vocabulary knowledge, students have to become familiar with the nature of academic language, including different grammars and discourse structures. Many of us have learned to do this unconsciously, but most of our students do not. So if our students are to become proficient learners in the content areas, it is not enough for them to learn the academic vocabulary. They must also become readers and users of academic language, which will entail some understanding of the typical functions, grammar, and discourse patterns in each content area. Such understanding has taken on greater importance now that most states have adopted the CCSS (NGA & CCSSO, 2010a). The CCSS place a new emphasis on academic language in several ways: They place shared responsibility for the language arts standards with science, social studies, and technical studies; they stress complex text; and they focus on argumentation with text-based evidence. So in this chapter we explore the nature of academic language—its characteristics, its purposes, and its grammar—and we describe instruction to help students learn and use such language (see Figure 2.1).

What Are Some Features of Academic Language?

Some characteristic features of academic language are that it explains complex ideas; it often includes abstract concepts; and it represents higher-order thinking. It is important to distinguish here between the general characteristics (functions) of academic language such as these, and the specific functions related to some purposes for which it is used. We look later at the purposes for which authors use academic language, often termed *academic discourses*, and reflected in typical *rhetorical structures*, such as persuasion or exposition.

Academic Language Explains Complex Ideas

There are many complex concepts in the different content areas (Schleppegrell, 2004), but there are also complex relationships. For example, students in science may be studying *homogeneous aqueous systems*. They need to understand the

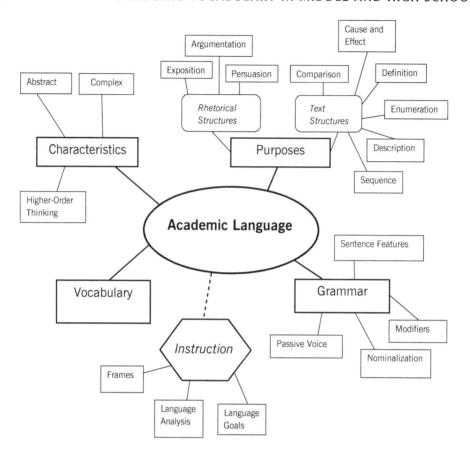

FIGURE 2.1. The nature of academic language. From Blachowicz, Fisher, Ogle, and Watts Taffe (2013). Copyright 2013 by The Guilford Press. Reprinted by permission.

importance of, and the difference between a *solvent* and a *solute*. Other terms might include *ionic compounds, polar covalent molecules,* and *positively charged ions.* Learning how all these terms are related, and the nature of aqueous systems, necessitates understanding the complex solution process. Similarly, there are complex relations in math between *angles, secants,* and *tangents.* In language arts we may ask students to describe how an author develops the characters in a novel. Likewise, it is common in history to study the causes of events (e.g., the causes of the U.S. Civil War). In order to describe complexity, therefore, we need a form of language that is initially unfamiliar to students and that it is our job to teach them.

Academic Language Often Includes Abstract Ideas

Many concepts and processes in the content areas are not only complex, but abstract. That is, they may deal with ideas and objects that are not available to the senses (they cannot be seen, heard, touched, etc.). Although *positive ions* and *negative ions* presumably take a physical form, understanding the meaning of the terms, the relationship between them, and the impact on our world requires a high level of abstract thinking. Mathematics is another subject where abstraction is often paramount; teaching algebra would be impossible without abstract thinking. Students in most content areas are asked to learn abstract concepts, such as *democracy*, and to engage in abstract thinking about a variety of relations among some of these concepts.

Academic Language Represents Higher-Order Thinking

Several taxonomies of thinking have been developed over the years, but the most commonly referenced is Bloom's (1956) taxonomy, which was revised by Lorin Anderson and his associates to include remembering, understanding, applying, analyzing, evaluating, and creating (Anderson & Krathwohl, 2001). This taxonomy has formed the basis for many others, and is often extended and adapted (see, e.g., Passig, 2003). Whichever way these higher-order thinking skills are described, Zwiers (2008) points out that there is often a disconnect between students' thinking in their social interactions (however complex these interactions may be) and their thinking in an academic context. Academic language functions to develop thinking, although there may be different emphases on particular forms of thinking in the different content areas.

Language, Context, and the Idea of Linguistic Registers

The idea of *linguistic registers* can help us understand how the lexical and grammatical features of academic language can change, depending on the purposes for which it is used. *Lexical features* are those related to words; *grammatical features* relate to sentence and other language structures. We all use different registers—for example, when talking to children, to friends, or to someone in authority. So a *register* is the constellation of lexical and grammatical features that we use in a particular context (Halliday & Hasan, 1989). For example, when meeting a child we might say, "Aren't you cute?", but when meeting an adult we are more likely to say, "How are you?" Similarly, when describing a seminar, a professor might tell a colleague, "It provided me with challenging ideas about schema theory for my research," but might tell a nonacademic friend, "It was good. I learned a lot." The rest of this book explores some of the lexical features of academic language—that is, the vocabulary used for different purposes in different content areas. We are suggesting that students can become more competent users of academic language if they are familiar with the registers typically used in a discipline. For example, when students study history in school, they tend to think of the information presented in school textbooks as "facts" or "the truth." As teachers, we can perpetuate this way of thinking by testing knowledge of these "facts." But we would like students to understand how historians select and interpret information in subjective and constructive ways. Learning about how historians use language for different purposes, and how it changes in relation to those purposes, can help develop this critical ability. In order to help them do so, we need to understand more about how registers work. As teachers, we need to talk about how knowledge is constructed through language in our different subject areas. It is necessary to make the link between the "content" and the language through which it is construed (Achugar, Schleppegrell, & Oteiza, 2007). Recently, this focus on the different discourses in the disciplines has come to be known as *disciplinary literacy* (Buehl, 2011), which can be thought of as the confluence of content knowledge with the ability to read, write, and think critically within the context of a discipline.

What Are the Purposes of Academic Language?

Academic discourses may differ in their purposes, and therefore their organizational features. We can categorize these features in two ways: *rhetorical mode* (e.g., exposition or persuasion) and *supporting text features* (e.g., description or classification). Butler, Bailey, Stevens, and Huang (2004) found that texts in science and texts in social studies differ in their predominant rhetorical modes:

> The difference in the writer's purpose from one subject area to another is clearly evident. . . . The science selections analyzed differ from the social studies selections in that they follow a more traditional expository form in which information is presented, explained, and then sometimes summarized in a fairly straightforward format. The social studies selections, on the other hand, use a narrative form to present information. That is, historical information often reads like a story, unfolding chronologically with details provided through the eyes of historical figures. (p. 85)

Butler and colleagues (2004) employed the term *narrative exposition* to characterize this mode in social studies. However, they found that science and social studies texts *all* use examples of the same supporting text features: *comparison, definition, description, enumeration, exemplification, explanation, labeling, paraphrase,* and *sequencing*. Since these features are common to more than one subject area, teachers from various areas of the curriculum could provide instruction in their use. We have always taught students that all reading and writing should be purposeful. We have emphasized reading to understand an author's purpose. What we may have not done so well is teach students how the discourse patterns that are the results of these purposes may differ between the subject areas.

Content-area reading texts frequently encourage us to think about text structure. They typically argue that we should teach five structures: *description, sequence, comparison–contrast, cause–effect,* and *problem–solution.* The recommendations are often accompanied by graphics, such as those shown in Figure 2.2.

In the United Kingdom, as part of the national literacy strategy, the use of *writing frames* is recommended for the exploration of various text structures. (We explore the use of frames in a later section.) We need to recognize that there is a difference between these macro-level structures and specific instances of comparison, definition, description, and so on, which may occur at the sentence or paragraph level. One of the CCSS Anchor Standards for Craft and Structure requires students to: "Analyze the structure of texts, including how specific sentences, paragraphs, and larger portions of text relate to each other and the whole" (NGA & CCSSO, 2010a, p. 35). Teachers in all the disciplines now bear the responsibility, along with language arts teachers, of developing students' ability to do such analyses.

How the Grammars of Academic Language Can Present Difficulties

Researchers at the Center for the Study of Evaluation at the University of California, Los Angeles, have done several studies on the nature of academic language. They have looked at texts, classroom discourse, and tests to analyze the nature of the language that students experience in schools, and how this language affects their learning (Bailey, Butler, LaFramenta, & Ong, 2004; Butler et al., 2004). In these studies, Bailey, Butler, and their colleagues have looked at some specific grammatical features: sentence type, clause type, passive verb forms, prepositional phrases, noun phrases, and participle modifiers. Since many of these features did not appear commonly in their analysis, for our exposition we are collapsing them into four categories: the use of complex sentence features, the use of the passive voice, the use of nominalization, and the use of modifiers and modals. These features will be common in the materials used for instruction.

The Use of Complex Sentence Features

Academic texts tend to have long, complex sentences. Consider this example:

> Fearful of struggles like this one, European leaders formed close associations, called alliances, with other countries, agreeing to supply military support to one another if necessary. (Bednarz et al., 2003, p. 387)

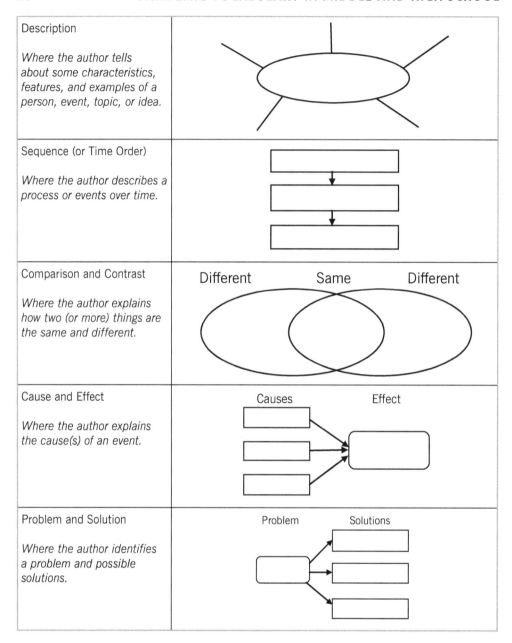

FIGURE 2.2. Five macrostructures in expository text. From Blachowicz, Fisher, Ogle, and Watts Taffe (2013). Copyright 2013 by The Guilford Press. Reprinted by permission.

In addition to causal links, definitional information, and some (probably) unfamiliar vocabulary, this sentence has an independent clause and two dependent clauses. That is, the complexity of the sentence could make accessing the content more difficult. Sentences like this, with subordinate clauses, represent hierarchical relationships that can lead to cognitive overload for those not comfortable with the content *or* the sentence structure.

There are various ways to classify the complexity of sentences. For our purposes, it is enough to know that a simple sentence contains one independent clause (e.g., *The temperature varies according to the seasons.*); a compound sentence contains two or more independent clauses joined by a conjunction or punctuation (e.g., *The positive charges form at the top of the cloud, and the negative charges form at the bottom of the cloud.*); and a complex sentence contains one or more dependent clauses, in addition to an independent clause (e.g., *If your hair stands on end or your skin starts to tingle, lightning may be about to strike.*). The literature (Schleppegrell, 2004; Zwiers, 2008) tells us that complex sentences are common in the content areas. The explanation is, of course, the grade level of the texts: The higher the grade level of the text, the greater the number of complex sentences (Schleppegrell, 2004). Although this information about the grammatical complexity of text is helpful and provides a warning of possible comprehension difficulties, we should also recognize that grammatically simple sentences are not necessarily simple in their content (e.g., *Mimicry is a type of protective coloration.*).

The Use of the Passive Voice

Many of us first experienced extensive use of the passive voice when studying science. The passive voice in academic texts is used to represent a supposedly objective point of view, based on facts rather than opinions. We were encouraged to use the passive voice in our lab reports, to practice the discourse conventions that occur in "scientific language." Passive voice relegates the true subject to the end of the sentence and is thus acted on, rather than acting. It takes the form (noun, object) (verb)(noun, subject). Consider this example: *Parts of an organism were replaced by minerals.* In this sentence, the true subject (*minerals*) is acted on, rather than acted. This issue of agency makes the passive voice difficult for some students to understand. Some learners, particularly those ELs whose primary language does not have a passive voice, may confuse the actor with the object of the action. Since passive-voice verb forms appear every four to five sentences in science and social studies texts (Butler et al., 2004), it would be appropriate for teachers in all disciplines to introduce the notion of passive voice and explain how it can clarify or confuse content in their fields.

One way to help students understand the passive voice is to compare it with the active voice in sentences that describe the same thing—for example, *James put his bag in the locker* and *The bag was put in the locker by James.* The students can act out the event, which makes it clear who is the actor and what is acted on. Similar cameos can be used to reinforce understanding of, and to help students practice the use of, the passive voice.

The Use of Nominalization

Nominalization is the process of expressing meanings that are more typically represented in verb, adverb, or adjective forms as nouns or noun phrases. In academic texts, nominalization often enables something that has been presented in a series of clauses to be distilled into one nominal element. Consider this example:

> Some polar molecular compounds are nonelectrolytes in the pure state, but *become electrolytes when they dissolve in water*. <u>*This process*</u> occurs because such compounds ionize in solution.

Another use of nominalization is to develop a chain of reasoning, as in this example:

> The ideas that are argued in this narrative are hard to believe. The *arguments* are loose and unappealing. The *looseness* makes the author's ideas difficult to follow. Their *lack of appeal* makes the document uninteresting.

Here, the verb in the first sentence is nominalized in the second one, and the two adjectives in the second sentence become nouns and the subjects of the next two sentences. So the process of nominalization across the paragraph lends coherence and structure to the argument. We know that students may struggle with pronominal referents (Bierwisch, 1983), and this additional complexity in terms of the cohesiveness of a text can be daunting. It may be important to help students to recognize how all these referents help to make a paragraph more comprehensible, and to point out instances in which they occur. But nominalization also condenses ideas, so that more may be expressed in a shorter space, which can lead to an even greater cognitive processing load.

When students read academic texts that use nominalization extensively, they have to understand more ideas per clause. They need opportunities to practice unpacking and translating these ideas, as well as recognizing why authors structure texts in a way that highlights new information and backgrounds to what has already been said. In addition, nominalization is often used with abstract concepts, so that readers may be challenged to remember many such relationships as they work their way through these texts.

Fang and Schleppegrell (2010) point out that while nominalization appears in all content areas, it can serve different functions in different disciplines. In science, nominalization can commonly help accrue meanings of a technical term, so that it can be used as a summary of an explanation sequence. In history, nominalization may be used commonly "to realize events as things so that historians can develop a chain of reasoning that at the same time embeds interpretation and judgment" (Fang & Schleppegrell, 2010, p. 590). For example, compare these two passages:

> If you look at bread mold through a microscope you can see tiny spheres sitting on top of thin stems. The sphere-shaped structures produce spores and are called *sporangia*. The "stems" are the bodies of the fungi and are termed *hyphae*.

> Toward the end of the 20th century senior workers, who had held jobs for a long time, thought they should have greater privileges than more recent hires. Seniority was often used as a criterion for job retention in times of restructuring and layoffs. The expectation of job security led to a lack of innovation as employers and entrepreneurs struggled with an aging work force.

An awareness of how nominalization can make texts in particular content areas more complex or more comprehensible will enable effective instruction to make such relationships more transparent to students.

The Use of Modifiers and Modal Verbs

Zwiers (2008) reminds us that nuances of meaning can be conveyed by modal verbs and qualifiers, and that such nuances are often problematic for EL students. Take, for example, *often, only, usually*, and similar adverbs. We may think that we use such modifiers extensively in conversation. We do, but in academic texts they may not be used in the same way. There are also modifiers we do use more commonly in oral language, such as *just* and *nearly*. Students are well aware of how modifiers work in their oral language, but it is appropriate to draw their attention to their use in academic text, especially when they are engaged in searching the Internet for information or are engaged in Web searches.

Another way that nuances of meaning are conveyed is through modal verbs—for example, *could, would, may, must*. Authors use modals to signal, for example, *intent, obligation, possibility*, and *conditionality*. The modal *would* is often used in conditional statements, such as *If . . . would*. This form asks students to think about cause and effect. All the disciplines ask students to employ this kind of thinking. Below, we talk about using frames such as *If . . . would* to develop students' understanding through discussion.

How Can We Promote Academic Language Learning?

Two important ways to develop academic language are through language analysis and through the use of frames. In this section, we describe the two approaches and include some related pedagogy.

Language Analysis

We have described how language can be analyzed at different levels: the word or lexical level, the grammatical level (sentence features, passive voice, and nominalization), and the discourse level (macro- and microstructures). Each of these levels of analysis can be introduced to the students through examples.

Once students have learned some of the language structures they may encounter in text, it may be appropriate to engage in a think-aloud to demonstrate how the structures work together to provide meaning. Too often, in our experience, teachers may engage in thinking aloud, and the students sit there looking puzzled because they have no idea what they are supposed to be observing. One way around this is to provide them with a way of marking the text. Using color-coded sticky notes or tabs is an easy way of doing this. The chart in Figure 2.3 gives an example.

The teacher reads a segment of the text aloud, stopping at various points to think aloud about the text structures as they occur. When the students hear the name of a structure, they put the appropriate-colored note or tab in their text. Students may initially need prompting to fully understand the task. Once they have done so, the students can engage in a think–pair–share, where they mark their texts individually, then meet with a partner to compare their markings. They might make a bar chart showing the number of structures that they have identified in a passage. This is a good way of showing students what structures are used most, and reminding them of all the ways they can engage effectively with text.

Text structure	Color
Comparison	Green
Definition	Blue
Description	Red
Enumeration	Yellow
Exemplification	Purple
Explanation	Orange
Sequence	Aqua

FIGURE 2.3. Think-aloud color code.

Here is an example of a think-aloud using an excerpt from a high school biology text. The text reads:

RELEASING ENERGY

Like all organisms, bacteria need a constant supply of energy. This energy is released by the processes of cellular respiration or fermentation or both. Organisms that require a constant supply of oxygen in order to live are called **obligate aerobes.** (Obligate means the organisms are obliged, or required, by their life processes to live only in that way.) *Mycobacterium tuberculosis,* the bacterium that causes tuberculosis, is an obligate aerobe.

Some bacteria, however, do not require oxygen and, in fact, may be killed by it! These bacteria are called **obligate anaerobes,** and they must live in the absence of oxygen. *Clostridium botulinum* is an obligate anaerobe found in soil. Because of its ability to grow without oxygen, it can grow in canned food that has not been properly sterilized. (Miller & Levine, 2006, p. 474)

The teacher's think-aloud may go something like this (the text as read aloud by the teacher is in *italics*):

"*Releasing energy.* OK, so this is the topic and tells me what I will be reading about.

"*Like all organisms, bacteria need a constant supply of energy. This energy is released by the processes of cellular respiration or fermentation or both.* So the first sentence is about bacteria needing energy. The second one tells me how this happens—respiration or fermentation. So everyone, have you marked description and explanation? OK—keep marking your text.

"*Organisms that require a constant supply of oxygen in order to live are called* **obligate aerobes.** This looks like a definition of what obligate aerobes are—organisms that need oxygen.

"(Obligate *means the organisms are obliged, or required, by their life processes to live only in that way.*) Great. They are explaining the meaning of *obligate.*

"*Mycobacterium tuberculosis, the bacterium that causes tuberculosis, is an obligate aerobe.* OK, this is an example of an obligate aerobe—I should be able to remember tuberculosis. So everyone, you should have marked definition, explanation, and exemplification for this part of the paragraph.

"*Some bacteria, however, do not require oxygen and, in fact, may be killed by it!* So some bacteria, in contrast, do need an absence of oxygen. I think there is a comparison coming.

"*These bacteria are called* **obligate anaerobes,** *and they must live in the absence of oxygen.* Yes—here is the comparison, which also defines what they are. I wonder if there will be an example?

"Clostridium botulinum is an obligate anaerobe found in soil. Because of its ability to grow without oxygen, it can grow in canned food that has not been properly sterilized. Mmm, sounds as if this example has something to do with botulism—nasty."

Different texts would need to be used to demonstrate all the structures. It is important for students to recognize that knowing which structures an author is using helps with understanding the text. This think-aloud and its extension into a think–pair–share provide an example of how modeling and discussion can help students analyze text structures. A similar process could occur with grammatical features, to teach students about sentence features, passive voice, nominalization, and modifiers/modals.

Teaching students to identify macrostructures can be accomplished through the use of graphic organizers, like those in Figure 2.1, applied to exemplar texts. Once again, modeling and discussion can be used to develop students' understanding. Some teachers also use these graphics to help students organize their thinking prior to writing. In some ways, they are frames. In the next section, we look at similar frames in more detail.

Fisher and Frey (2010) suggest another way to use language analysis. They recommend making explicit for EL students the language purposes for a lesson, as well as content purposes. After surveying teachers of K–12 EL students in California, they developed a framework that examines purposes related to vocabulary, language structure, and language function. They looked at statements about what teachers said were the language purposes of their lessons. Examples of these language purpose statements from social studies included the following (Fisher & Frey, 2010, p. 323):

Vocabulary—Name the routes and explorers on a map.
Language Structure—Sequence the steps of food production using the signal words *first, then, next,* and *finally.*
Language Function—Justify in a paragraph the ways fire was used for hunting, cooking, and warmth by citing three examples.

Fisher and Frey found three types of language structure statements that the teachers in their survey used: (1) specific grammar and syntax rules that students should practice; (2) signal words that are common in academic English; and (3) sentence frames representing certain language structures. They did not specify which functions teachers reported using, but gave examples from other researchers, such as *analyze, compare, describe, observe, summarize, persuade, sequence,* and *evaluate.* They concluded that their framework is suitable for providing purposes in lessons for EL students. We think that they are probably suitable for all students.

Using Sentence Frames

The use of language frames that exemplify particular language patterns has been recommended in relation to students' writing (Wray, 2001), but is now also being suggested for use with students' oral language (Fisher & Frey, 2010). Frames can take a variety of forms. Carrier and Tatum (2006) extend the idea of word walls to using sentence walls. They argue that for EL students, "sentence walls provide a visual scaffold of language (e.g., phrases, sentences) to help students communicate in classroom discussions about content" (p. 286). They suggest that frames can be posted on classroom walls for students to refer to when talking about content. For example, question frames might include the following:

What happens when . . . ?
How does . . . ?
What causes . . . to . . . ?

Carrier and Tatum also suggest sentence frames about specific content for statements to use in discussion—a type of sentence completion task.

A shift in equilibrium occurs when. . . .
Monocots have . . . , while dicots have. . . .

In order to construct such frames, it is useful to think about "What do I want the students to say about [*releasing energy*], and how do I want them to say it?" They further recommend that sentence frames such as these should be linked to key vocabulary as part of a content-focused word wall. Donnelly and Roe (2010) recommend introducing such frames through modeling, group practice, and then individual application.

Ross, Fisher, and Frey (2009, p. 29) developed six categories of sentence frames for argumentation in science, with examples of frames for students to use in each category:

1. *Making a claim*: I noticed . . . when . . . ; I compared . . . and . . .
2. *Providing evidence*: I know that . . . is . . . because . . . ; Based on . . . , I think . . .
3. *Asking for evidence*: I have a question about . . . ; What causes . . . to . . . ?
4. *Offering a counterclaim*: I disagree with . . . because . . . ; In my opinion . . .
5. *Inviting speculation*: I wonder what would happen if . . . ; We want to test . . . to find out if . . .
6. *Reaching consensus*: I agree with . . . because . . .

These frames are designed for use in conversation, and only some are included here. For the full list, we refer you to the original Ross and colleagues (2009) article.

Zwiers and Crawford (2011) also have examples in their text, along with many other ideas to develop effective academic conversations. There are numerous examples of sentence frames for different disciplines on the Internet, for example, *www.mckeecths.org/resources/sentence-frames*. Later in this book, we suggest the use of sentence frames with other discussion routines.

Concluding Thoughts

In this age of new literacies (Baker, 2010), we need to consider that students will be engaging with multimedia texts. These multisemiotic texts make meaning in a variety of ways that go beyond traditional written texts, and we will have to consider the many ways that they make meaning in the disciplines. Sentence and text structure, grammars and rhetorical structures, may be only part of what we need to teach students. In fact, even the ways we teach students about academic language will be influenced by digital media and other forms of new literacies. We know that science and math textbooks exemplify the integration of visual and print information, and now this has been extended with virtual labs, demonstrations, presentations, video, and other forms of digital text. The texts include links that a teacher can assign for instruction or practice. We will explore some of this later in the book. This is an exciting time, when our students may be teaching us about some texts, while we teach them about others.

CHAPTER 3

Understanding Effective Vocabulary Instruction in Grades 6–12

Notes from a teacher study group on responses to the question "What do we do with vocabulary?":

> JESSE: I am getting really confused by all these academic vocabulary strategies we are hearing about for our content classes. I feel like I have a cookbook, but no plan about what to cook and when to cook it!

> MARTA: I want to have a better idea of the research base for teaching vocabulary in general before I can tell what fits where.

> JOE: Now the big push is for academic vocabulary, but I don't feel like I have general vocabulary under control. *Is* there "general" vocabulary research?

The vignette above introduces the goals of this chapter. We know that knowledge of academic vocabulary contributes to school success (Townsend, Filippini, Collins, & Biancarosa, 2012). It is also clear that gaps in academic vocabulary have been strongly associated with lack of school success for both monolingual and bilingual students (Garcia, 1991; Riddle-Buly & Valencia, 2002). In the preceding chapters, we introduced you to ideas, research, and questions about academic vocabulary and academic language that can help you begin to build your own knowledge base. As a bridge to the rest of this book, which focuses on instruction in specific content domains, this chapter provides you with an overview of what educational researchers and practitioners know and think about effective *general* vocabulary instruction. If you already know a lot about this topic, you might want to skim the headings in this chapter to see where you want to focus. If you are a newcomer to thinking about vocabulary instruction, this chapter will help you build background. We start with a brief overview of some of the key research, resulting in four basic understandings that underpin good vocabulary instruction. We follow this with a description of the four essential components of comprehensive vocabulary instruction and the roles of key players, including parents and principals as well as teachers and students.

The Background Builders

The last two decades have seen an explosion of interest in vocabulary instruction—an interest that builds on years of research and practical experimentation. If you are interested in building your background in this research, the second volume of the *Handbook of Reading Research* (Barr, Kamil, Mosenthal, & Pearson, 1991) contains two foundational chapters on vocabulary: one dealing with vocabulary processes (Anderson & Nagy, 1991) and a second with vocabulary development (Beck & McKeown, 1991). These same two topics were updated in chapters (Blachowicz & Fisher, 2000; Nagy & Scott, 2000) in the subsequent third volume of the handbook, as well as in a chapter of the *Handbook of Teaching the English Language Arts* (Baumann, Kame'enui, & Ash, 2003) and in other comprehensive volumes (e.g., Farstrup & Samuels, 2008), including some that focus on these issues in middle and secondary schools (Nagy & Townsend, 2012; Shanahan & Shanahan, 2008).

Happily, literacy educators have surveyed this landscape of research and attempted to interpret it for practitioners in research-based application volumes focused on instruction (Beck et al., 2013; Blachowicz & Fisher, 2014; Frey & Fisher, 2009; Graves, 2006; Hiebert & Kamil, 2005; Kame'enui & Baumann, 2012; Lubliner & Scott, 2008). Studies specific to upper-level learners have also described interventions and instruction (August & Gray, 2010; Lesaux, Kieffer, Faller, & Kelley, 2010).

There are also many short and specific articles that present overviews of the landscape. Key facets of study have included the nature of vocabulary acquisition, including the wide array of information needed for truly "knowing" a word (Nagy, Herman, & Anderson, 1985); characteristics associated with effective instruction of individual word meanings (Mezynski, 1983; Stahl & Fairbanks, 1986); strategies that individuals use to determine the meanings of unknown words encountered in reading and the ways they can be successfully taught (Baumann, Edwards, Boland, Olejnik, & Kame'enui, 2003); characteristics of and differences in vocabulary acquisition across students (Biemiller & Slonim, 2001; Hart & Risley, 1995); and focuses on learning in content area classes (Fang & Schleppergrell, 2010; Snow, Lawrence & White, 2009; Zweirs, 2008).

The practical implication of all this information is that in order to address the complex, multidimensional nature of word learning—and academic word learning specifically—we need to approach vocabulary comprehensively (Hiebert & Kamil, 2005; Stahl & Nagy, 2006; Watts Taffe, Blachowicz, & Fisher, 2009).

This leads us to some key concepts that are critical to structuring good instruction.

Four Basic Understandings

Four things that flow out of this research are "basics" to understanding good vocabulary instruction:

1. The term *vocabulary* has multiple meanings.
2. Vocabulary learning is incremental.
3. Vocabulary learning is both incidental and intentional.
4. Vocabulary instruction is *everyone's* responsibility.

The Term *Vocabulary* Has Multiple Meanings

Everyone has many types of "vocabularies." We have already introduced the idea that academic vocabulary is a special kind of vocabulary, and this idea is well developed in the following chapters. When we use the term *vocabulary*, sometimes we are talking about the words that students use in speech (oral vocabulary) but are not yet able to decode in written text (reading vocabulary). Sometimes they can understand a word they hear (listening vocabulary) but cannot use that same word in speech or writing. Figure 3.1 shows a handy way of organizing what we know about types of vocabulary.

Students' receptive vocabularies are often far more advanced than their expressive ones, especially in the early grades. In fact, Biemiller and Slonim (2001) propose that students' receptive vocabularies can be at least two grade levels higher than their expressive vocabularies. So when we read to children, we can use more difficult vocabulary to stretch their receptive abilities. Expressive use of words is often considered more difficult than receptive use. For reading or listening, students often just need a general idea of a word and can use syntactic and semantic context clues to help them understand; to use it in speech or writing, more precision is required in both meaning and usage. In school, we want to develop all four of these areas: oral receptive vocabulary (for listening), oral expressive vocabulary (for speaking), reading (receptive) vocabulary, and writing (expressive) vocabulary.

	Receptive	Expressive
Oral	Listening	Speaking
Written	Reading	Writing

FIGURE 3.1. We all have different types of vocabulary.

Vocabulary Learning Is Incremental

Most researchers agree that word learning is not an all-or-nothing proposition, like a switch that turns a light on or off. A better metaphor is that of a dimmer switch, which gradually supplies an increasingly rich supply of light. For example, children learn the word *daddy, papi,* or *papa* and begin to apply it to all men, sometimes with humorous results. For older students, this might be signaled by a student writing a riddle saying, "Mom, it's the mathematical version of *whole* I'm talking about, not the other version of *hole*." Essential to this riddle is a developing knowledge of homophones, as well as an understanding that particular words served specific functions in different disciplines.

This commonly observed process of incremental learning mirrors research suggesting that learners move from not knowing a word, to being somewhat acquainted with it, to a deeper, richer, more flexible word knowledge that allows them to use new words in many modalities of expression (Graves, 1986; McKeown & Beck, 1988). Repeated encounters with words in a variety of rich oral and written contexts provide experiences and clues to the words' meanings and limitations that build over time, helping to develop and change learners' mental structures for the words' meanings (Eller, Pappas & Brown, 1988; Nagy, 1988; Vosniadou & Ortony, 1983). Meaningful use, review, and practice that calls on students to use vocabulary in authentic ways are all essential for developing rich and full word knowledge.

Because the number of encounters needed to learn a word depends on learner characteristics such as background experience and knowledge, interest, engagement and motivation, characteristics of the words to be learned (such as concreteness or abstractness), and contextual characteristics, there is no definitive research that can be cited to answer the question "Well, how many repetitions are needed?" Studies of young children and of older ELs report ranges from 10 to 40 encounters for infants and toddlers as necessary (Bergelson & Swingley 2013) and 6 to 20 meaningful repetitions for older students and ELs (Pigada & Schmitt 2006).

Yet other studies also suggest that "fast mapping" can take place, making an initial inference about the meaning of a word in only one or two encounters (Medina, Snedeker, Trueswell, & Gleitman, 2011). Parents note that their children often learn forbidden words with only one exposure! Our observational research in upper-grade classrooms implementing a comprehensive model documented more than 25 observed encounters with each target word over a 1-week period. And these were only times when we heard the words highlighted orally or in discussion with the group, or encountered in assigned reading or review during our 1-hour daily observations. One important aspect of these encounters is that the contexts were varied, not a rote repetition of the same context. The student encountered the word in teacher preparation for the unit of study; met it in text; and used it in partner work, in class discussion, and in oral presentation and writing. This did not include any encounters with the words when we were not present or in student individual work, reading, writing, or homework (Blachowicz, Bates, & Cieply 2011).

Vocabulary Learning Is Both Incidental and Intentional

Incidental Learning

Rich exposure to words, such as that provided by wide reading, helps students construct and retain meaningful personal contexts for words (Whittlesea, 1987). For example, reading the word *sheath* in one of *The Hunger Games* novels (Collins, 2008) makes it meaningful in the way a dictionary definition or in an isolated sentence never could. Specific events in the novels help the learner note that a *sheath* is a container that it is small and light enough to be carried by Katniss, and that it has an opening that can store arrows for her bow. Readers who have read these engaging books have no trouble conceptualizing or remembering the term *sheath*.

Estimates suggest that school-age students from primary through high school learn an average of 3,000–4,000 words per year (D'Anna, Zechmeister, & Hall, 1991; Nagy & Herman, 1987), although some researchers have suggested that this average varies widely, depending on students' background of home and school experiences (Becker, 1977; White, Graves, & Slater, 1990). The term *learning* in most of these studies refers to growth in familiarity of recognition for certain frequently encountered words, as measured on wide-scale tests or through research studies such as those carried out for *The Living Word Vocabulary* (Dale & O'Rourke, 1976). This rapid and large growth suggests that a significant amount of vocabulary learning takes place through incidental or environmental learning (e.g., wide reading, discussion, listening, and exposure to the mass media), rather than from direct instruction. For instance, students who know the word *sweeper* as a position in soccer have typically learned that through play and experience, not through books or watching World Cup matches on TV. Similarly, students in California during the summer of 2014 heard words such as *drought* and *reservoir* as newscasters, environmental scientists, and neighbors discussed the extreme state of drought the state was in. We learn from interacting with and using words in all sorts of meaningful contexts, and it is important that the classroom supports and builds on this kind of learning.

Intentional Learning and Instruction

But vocabulary can also be learned and taught intentionally, through explicit or implicit instruction. From the popularity of *Reader's Digest* "How to Increase Your Word Power" exercises in the 1950s and 1960s, to the executive word power programs advertised in airline magazines, deliberate study has always been part of adult self-improvement models. For school-age students, research suggests that the intentional teaching of specific words and word-learning strategies can build students' vocabularies (Lesaux et al., 2010; Tomeson & Aarnoutse, 1998), as well as improve reading comprehension of texts containing those words (McKeown, Beck, Omanson, & Pople, 1985; Stahl & Fairbanks, 1986).

Planning for Incidental and Intentional Learning

Teachers with whom we have worked found it useful to think of three ways in which the teacher can think about vocabulary instruction: (1) *Flooding* students with words, (2) *Fast* teaching, and (3) *Focused* teaching. From research by Nagy and others that we discussed earlier, we know that intentional instruction cannot account for all the words students learn. For that reason, classrooms should be flooded with words related to topics of study and ways to create related sets of these words so that maximal incidental learning can take place.

   1. **Flood.** Flooding the environment of students with words for incidental learning is an important aspect that we discuss later in this chapter. Both fast and focused teacher instruction complements this learning environment.

   2. **Fast.** You can use fast instruction for terms where an easy definition or analogy will build on knowledge the students already have. We know that short definitional word explanations can do the trick when the concept is familiar but the term is not (Baumann et al., 2003; Kame'enui & Baumann, 2012; McKeown et al., 1985; Pany, Jenkins, & Schreck 1982). Fast-paced instruction identifies the word, provides a synonym, gives an example of use, and then asks students to provide their own connection or synonym. When words are *almost* alike, a short feature analysis, word laddering, or semantic decision question ("Would you want a microscope or a periscope to check the horizon? Why or why not?") can help students access an unfamiliar word quickly.

   3. **Focus.** Use focused instruction for words where deeper, semantically rich teaching of a new concept is required, such as the word *democracy* or *symbiosis*. These are easy words to memorize a definition for, but each represents a rich and complex topic that continues to grow in a network of meaning we refine as we move into a more global society. This demands instruction using both definitional and contextual information, multiple exposures, close reading in many contexts, and deep levels of processing, calling on students to discuss and use the word with teacher and peers to develop a rich base for word meaning (Graves, 1986; Mezynski, 1983; Nagy & Scott, 2000; Stahl & Fairbanks, 1986) and reading comprehension (Baumann, 2009; Elleman, Endia, Morphy, & Compton, 2009).

These three dimensions can help you fine-tune instruction. First, you need to decide whether a word can be taught easily or whether it needs more instruction. Imagine a group of students who are familiar with the term *crown*. Teaching the meaning of the word *diadem* won't be too difficult. They already have the concept of a crown and are learning only a new label for a related term. Fast instruction with a picture and brief discussion of synonyms might be enough, and ensuring repeated context through reading and use in discussion will help the word stick.

For the same students, however, the word *nostalgia* would probably be harder to teach. This is an abstract concept that might not be too familiar to teens, and the teacher would have to help the students, through discussion and work with the words (focused instruction), to establish a network of related concepts, such as longing, the past, and so forth. So it makes sense to think about "knowing" a word as a continuous process that can be affected by meaningful encounters with words and by instruction aimed at helping the learner develop a network of understanding. The instructional situation that the teacher selects will vary depending both on the frameworks of knowledge the learners already have and the importance of the term to the task at hand. For students whose heritage languages are not English, or those who struggle with reading, this instruction can be even more critical.

Vocabulary Instruction Is *Everyone's* Responsibility

A last basic understanding is the need for schoolwide commitment to developing vocabulary. "We're all in this together" is a good slogan to describe school communities that know attention to vocabulary is an important part of their job. Parents and families, schools, and principals, as well as teachers and students, all have important parts to play in building strong vocabularies for students.

Parents

Parents are our students' first teachers, and Hart and Risley's (1995) landmark study of preschool vocabulary learning highlighted the role of parental input. They found that children from homes with less frequent talk had significantly fewer words in their oral vocabularies when they entered school. Graves (1986) has suggested that the gap in kindergarten between the most and least verbally advantaged students is about 3,000 words and grows as students approach middle and high school. These studies clearly demonstrate the importance of parent–child talk—both in frequency *and* in the number of words to which parents expose their children—for vocabulary learning.

It is equally clear that, as students grow older, continued talk with them (not at them) is critical to their vocabulary development. Discussion of current events around the dinner table or by watching the nightly news brings relevance to the vocabulary of world events and citizenship. Involvement in the life of their communities, of the broader society, travel and other experiences each bring new ideas and words into the mix. Talk along with shared life experiences gives them meaningful and personal exposure to the richness of vocabulary that we use to describe it.

Although talk is essential, reading is also a powerful source for general vocabulary development (Cunningham & Stanovich, 1998) and is especially critical in the adolescent years when there is a documented decline in personal reading by teens (Common Sense Media, 2014). So getting students to read more is often the most crucial thing a parent can do. Teachers can help by giving providing guidelines and cautions that can help parents navigate the tricky world of raising adolescent learners.

Some ideas for parents of middle and high school readers are listed in Figure 3.2.

The Principal

Education research has firmly established that the principal is a key collaborator in motivating teachers, implementing a solid curriculum, and maintaining a positive

---

IDEAS FOR ENCOURAGING ADOLESCENT READERS

- Set an example and let them see you read books, magazines, blogs, and websites for your own pleasure and information. Make it interactive by talking with them about what you are reading and learning.
- Make sure there is a variety of reading material available to them. What the statistics on teen reading for pleasure don't capture is the amount of online and magazine reading.
- Let them choose, and don't criticize. Avoid the word *classic* when describing a book you might recommend. At the same time, you can help them find well-written books related to their choices to extend their range.
- Think outside the box with audiobooks, graphic novels, podcasts, and other types of reading materials and media.
- Read some books and magazines recommended for teens. Reading the series they are interested in or reading magazines they like can build your own knowledge base of popular culture and give you things to talk about.
- Acknowledge your teen's interests by sharing articles you find in newspapers and magazines and locating magazines that support these interests. A magazine subscription related to their interest is a great gift.
- Help make time for reading on vacation, by having home reading time, by doing beach reading, by visiting bookstores and libraries to browse. Try to balance tech time with some no-tech time.

FIGURE 3.2. Guidelines for parents.

school environment (National Association of Secondary School Principals, 2013); this is something teachers and parents all understand. A principal working in collaboration with teachers and other educational personnel can affect hundreds, or in the case of some larger high schools, thousands of students each year. Just as "one-shot" professional development has limited impact, so too do "one-teacher, one-year" vocabulary programs. The whole school needs to acknowledge the importance of building vocabularies and work together to create an emphasis across the grades.

The principal affects this, first of all, by engaging a school's teachers in professional development and study groups to build their content knowledge about good vocabulary instruction. The principal can help to build a culture of learning that celebrates word play and highlights the connection between word knowledge and opportunity/power/freedom. Highlighting the important role that vocabulary plays in all the CCSS can knit these initiatives together (Blachowicz & Baumann, 2013). There is an abundance of support materials for such study, including the teacher-focused resources we have mentioned above (see "The Background Builders"); materials specifically designed for study groups (Dimino & Taylor, 2009; Graves, 2009); and "action packs" for teachers and coaches (Blachowicz & Cobb, 2007), which share specific ideas for curricular improvement.

Besides planning focused and ongoing staff development in vocabulary instruction, the principal's best role is as "cheerleader" for vocabulary. Finding ways to highlight vocabulary and have fun with words as a whole school can help everyone—students, teachers, and parents—become enthusiastic.

One principal also has a great tool for stimulating word learning: the public address system. Haggard (1982), in a study of word learning among middle school students, was perplexed by the fact that middle schoolers in one school all knew the meaning of the word *behoove*—not a common word even in most adults' vocabularies! She traced the learning back to the day before winter break, when the principal announced, "It behooves everyone to clean out his or her locker before the break. Things left in lockers will be thrown away." The students thought that *behoove* was one of the funniest words they had ever heard. That week, the teacher heard "It behooves you to get your feet off my chair," and "It behooves you to give me back my pencil." Funny-sounding words intrigue students; the use of creative and interesting vocabulary for daily announcements adds to incidental learning and reminds students that vocabulary is important.

In a more intentional way, one principal has students from one classroom each week announce four "special" words they are studying each Monday. The students post these four words in four public places in the school. For example, one week the word *informative* was posted on the library door, *perspire* in the gym, *selection* on the vending machine, and *linoleum* on the floor by the office. A manila folder was placed on the classroom door, and students could drop in their ideas about why certain words were in certain places. On Friday, the students would explain their reasoning about word placement and draw one idea out of the envelope. If the student drawn had an appropriate explanation, he or she received a ticket that entitled the student to certain school benefits.

The principal also needs to make sure that teachers across the school have resources needed to both stimulate interest in words and teach new vocabulary. These resources should include high-interest books for independent reading on all topics of interest to adolescents, along with periodical subscriptions. Other obvious resources are dictionaries, including "learner" dictionaries, games, books, and puzzle software. One principal bought small whiteboards for each classroom. On the whiteboards, each class posted a few choice words they were studying each week. All the trips down the halls became learning experiences for students. When they passed another group of students on the way to lunch or gym, they could ask about any words they saw. Besides providing good professional development and resources to teachers, the principal has great potential for highlighting vocabulary learning and use as a schoolwide goal.

Implementing a balanced and comprehensive approach to vocabulary can pay off across grades and subject areas. Teachers and students are at the heart of this process, and we examine their contributions and actions as we discuss what a comprehensive program looks like.

The Comprehensive Vocabulary Program

The diagram in Figure 3.3 illustrates the components of a comprehensive vocabulary program (Baumann et al., 2011, 2013; Graves, 2006). We now discuss each of these components: (1) providing rich and varied language experiences; (2) teaching specific vocabulary intentionally; (3) teaching word-learning strategies; and (4) fostering word consciousness.

Providing Rich and Varied Language Experiences

James Britton (1993) has noted, "Reading and writing float on a sea of language." This wonderful comment gives us a great visual metaphor for thinking about the first component of a comprehensive vocabulary program. In Figure 3.3, you can see that this "sea" of language surrounds everything else we do in vocabulary teaching.

We know that students learn words incidentally by reading independently (Cunningham, 2005; Kim & White, 2008; Swanborn & de Glopper, 1999), by listening to texts read aloud, and through exposure to enriched oral language (Dickinson

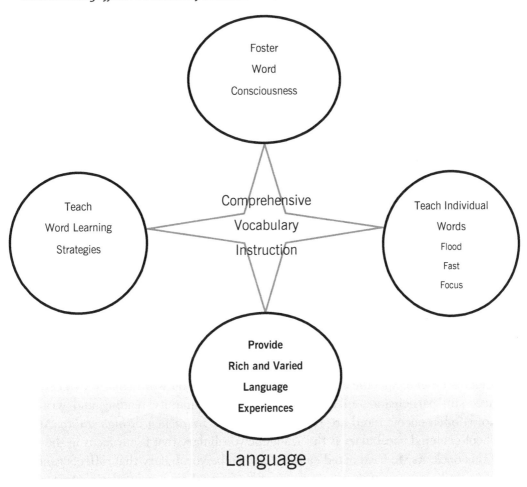

FIGURE 3.3. The four essential components of comprehensive vocabulary instruction. From Blachowicz, Fisher, Ogle, and Watts Taffe (2013). Copyright 2013 by The Guilford Press. Reprinted by permission.

& Smith, 1994). We know that students acquire vocabulary in an accelerated fashion through read-alouds when teachers or caregivers provide elaboration (definitional and contextual information) on words in the texts (Blachowicz & Obrochta, 2007; Bus, van IJzendoorn, & Pellegrini, 1995; van Kleeck, Stahl, & Bauer, 2003). We also know that interactive read-alouds are doubly important for the learning and retention of older students who are ELs or struggling readers (Serafini & Giorgias, 2003). And the sea of language Britton speaks of has become even richer for students through technology.

What's in this "sea"? It's the environment in which word learning takes place. Teachers need to:

- Ensure time and support for regular personal reading of on-level texts. Teachers can model book selection and do book talks to stimulate interest in different genres, authors, and formats (electronic texts, graphic novels, manga, etc.).
- Provide time and support for meaningful student discussion and writing. Many students need to receive modeling and support for *how* to talk about a text or issue (Evans, 2002). This support may be as basic as taking turns, looking at the speaker, and giving some sort of response; or it may be more elaborate, such as the use of PRC2 (Ogle & Correa-Kovtun, 2010), content reading or using discussion frames (Blachowicz et al., 2011), or charting for character traits (Manyak, 2007). We elaborate on these instructional approaches in later chapters. Similarly, in their writing, students need to be supported with graphics, planning, and other models to begin using elaborated vocabulary.
- Explore and support the many technological means for rich communication—synchronous and asynchronous discussions, Skype, FaceTime, games like Heads Up—to mention only a few.

Teaching Specific Vocabulary Intentionally

Students deserve specific and intentional instruction on words that they need for successful participation in home, school, and community reading and writing. Words often encountered are referred to as *high frequency* or *high utility*. More school-centered vocabulary is the academic vocabulary that is our focus in the rest of this book. As we have noted earlier, this can be vocabulary that reflects general school tasks (e.g., *summarize*); or it might be focused on a particular content area, such as math (*diameter*), social studies (*Confederacy* or *emigration/nationalism/ Manifest Destiny*), science (*symbiosis*), literature (*genre*), or the arts (*Expressionism*). There are also domains of student interest that have specific vocabularies all their own, such as basketball (*cager*), surfing (*boogie board*), graphic reading materials (*manga*), yoga (*bikram*), gaming (*nerf*, and it's not a ball!), and so forth.

General Instructional Framework for Teaching Individual Words

There are many different ways to teach individual words, but teachers need to make sure students:

1. Hear and see, hear and say the word. Pronunciation can call up oral vocabulary if students know the word in speech.
2. Hear the word in context (usage and meaning).
3. Get to a definition. Teachers can elicit definitions from students and restate them or provide a "student-friendly" definition.

4. Make a personal connection and use the word in a meaningful way.
5. Participate in a semantic decision task and explain reasoning. (Note that 4 and 5 can be done in reverse order.)
6. Record. This can be independent work in a vocabulary notebook, such as constructing a "four-square" for each vocabulary word (with the word in one square, a definition in the second, an example in the third, and a picture as a visual clue in the fourth square).

It's essential for students to revisit the words later in the lesson, and to continue encountering them in print and discussion, reading, research, inquiry, and writing.

Let's see what this looks like if a teacher wants to teach the meaning of *buffet* (meaning "to hit repeatedly"). First, the word is placed on the board, and the teacher leads the students through the steps:

1. "Let's say it . . . it's not boo/fay, it's buff/it." (See/say.)
2. "Here's an example. When there is a windstorm, the tree branches buffet my roof and knock off shingles." (Hear the word in context.)
3. "What could it mean?" (Get to a definition.) The teacher elicits or gives or restates a meaning: "Right, it means 'hit.'" The teacher then says, "Let's check," and has students give/find definition to confirm (optional if time).
4. "Turn and talk with your partner, and use *buffet* in a sentence about something you remember or imagine." (Make a personal connection.) The teacher can then give feedback on usage.
5. "Let me ask you a question: Would I want you to buffet others in the classroom? Why or why not?" (Participate in a decision task and explain reasoning.)
6. "OK, record *buffet* in your word book/sheet, and add a synonym or short definition and a picture that helps you remember the meaning." (Record.) The teacher can use this as meaningful seatwork or homework.

These steps are negotiable and can be organized according to what the students already know, but they will help establish a basic routine for teaching individual words.

Teaching Word-Learning Strategies

Students need to be able to strategically use context, as well as prefixes, suffixes, and roots, to infer the meanings of new words. This requires them to learn the meanings of prefixes and suffixes, and to engage in strategies for applying these generative elements to new words. They should also learn to use context clues when encountering unknown words (Baumann et al., 2003; Baumann, Ware, & Edwards,

2007; Fukkink & de Glopper, 1998). Word parts are particularly important in the content areas and will be highlighted in each content chapter.

Fostering Word Consciousness

If the prior three components are being approached in an engaging manner, we teachers will have a head start on developing students' *word consciousness* (sometimes called *word awareness*)—that is, their understanding of how words work and their flexibility in using words (Graves, 2006; Nagy, 2005; Scott et al., 2012). We need to nurture our students' interest in words and their meanings, along with an appreciation of how writers and speakers choose and use specific words and phrases to convey different shades of meaning. We want them to have a playful and joyful pleasure in an interesting word or turn of phrase, and to appreciate the many ways they can use our rich and flexible language in their own speech and writing. Some highlights of building word consciousness are discussed below.

Classroom Environment

The environment for word learning must be engaging. Having word games, books, puzzle-making software, and time to use all these will help students become word lovers. Word walls, student work, and other displays also emphasize that vocabulary learning is fun and important. Along with time devoted to reading and writing as described earlier, time for fun is important.

Materials

Having a selection of different dictionaries, including topical ones (e.g., *Dictionary of Dance, The Automobile Dictionary*) and electronic resources makes it easy for students to pursue words related to their various interests. Also, learner dictionaries—those meant for students who have heritage languages other than English (e.g., the Longman Learner Dictionaries), are essential for every classroom.

Models

Students need to hear and read models of good language use. Teachers themselves, of course, are powerful models of spoken language, and videos of many eloquent public speakers reading to children are accessible today. The Rev. Jesse Jackson reading Dr. Seuss's (1960) *Green Eggs and Ham* (*www.youtube.com/watch?v= DPy2alWEZ-U*) is a favorite with students, and YouTube makes many other powerful speakers available to the classroom.

Books used as mentor texts for student writing and as models of fine word choice abound, from the works of J. K. Rowling to those of Rick Riordan and Stephen King for older students. Cunningham and Stanovich (1998) point out that even primary-level books have a more elevated level of vocabulary than the language most college-educated adults use in daily life. For ELs, poetry can be a particularly rich source of conversation about word choice.

Scott and colleagues (2012) have developed methods for discussing authors' language use in ways that influence student writing. Their "Gift of Words" model engages students in selecting and sharing fine language use throughout the year and incorporating ideas into their own writing.

Introducing Word Relationships

Every curriculum introduces the basic relationships of words as synonyms and words as antonyms. Understanding these two key relationships is a good starting point for becoming familiar with the ways words relate to one another. But there are many more relationships that form the foundation of an educated person's vocabulary. For example, the Wordle (*www.wordle.net*), or graphic "word cloud" shown in Figure 3.4, was made by students listing their favorite word relationships.

In short, students develop word consciousness by engaging in playful language activities; by making visual representations of categories, webs, and maps (such as the Wordle in Figure 3.4); and by exploring the words accomplished authors and speakers use (Graves & Watts-Taffe, 2002; Nagy, 2005; Scott, Jamieson-Noel, & Asselin, 2003). Graphic mapping of complex word relationships, use of semantic

FIGURE 3.4. Example of a Wordle.

organizers, word webs, word ladders, and the like make this learning concrete, as do personal word recollections, tablet computer or cell phone records, and other visual representations.

Promoting Students' Independent Word Learning

Students also need to become responsible for monitoring their own word learning. The CCSS stress teaching students to use frequency of occurrence, highlighting, headings, diagrams, visual clues and other signals to identify important words for study. Beyond words selected and presented by teachers in disciplinary classes, students also need to identify words that they want to learn for their own knowledge. Jiminez (1997) found middle schoolers became more engaged in vocabulary learning, and learned more vocabulary when they were able self-selected words for study. Other research on self-selection (Fisher Blachowicz, & Smith, 1991; Ruddell & Shearer, 2002) revealed that, in literary disciplines, students often choose harder words and learn a significant number of them when encouraged to self-select entries for their own word collections.

Learning to use electronic references is also an important part of student independence. Science teachers in one of our projects kept one classroom computer open to a reference page for an interactive science dictionary with accessible explanations open at all times for students to consult when needed. The used their Smart Board to display terms when a lot of students were confused, gradually turning that job over to a different student each day. Turning more over to the students helped them on the road to independence.

Concluding Thoughts

In this chapter, we have rounded out your introduction to academic vocabulary, academic language, and comprehensive vocabulary instruction. This provides a foundation of background knowledge for your immersion in the more specific disciplinary chapters that follow.

CHAPTER 4

Teaching Academic Vocabulary in the English Language Arts

While speaking with middle and high school English language arts (ELA) teachers in preparation to write this chapter, "I wish I did that better" was a common refrain. As a high school English and reading teacher myself (Laura), I too struggled to determine how much time I should devote to focused word learning. Was I teaching enough words? Was I spending enough time introducing students to words they might encounter in college entrance exams? Was I helping students understand the power that the right word can have in our social lives, in our written lives, in our democracy?

The fact is this: We owe it to our students to immerse them in words, to introduce them to the power that words can have in our lives, to the joy that comes from exploring the complex and often quirky intricacies of the English language. Subsequently, this chapter will introduce key understandings and challenges of teaching vocabulary in upper-grade ELA courses, review the CCSS guidelines for vocabulary, and explore the instructional strategies and resources that have the most promise for supporting adolescents' growing understanding of word and language use. Throughout the chapter, we share engaging, innovative approaches that individual teachers are using to support both incidental and intentional word learning in their classrooms.

ELA Instruction and Language/Cultural Identity

As English teachers invite students on a journey through language from different historical periods, cultures and genres, they are in a unique place to celebrate the shifting purposes of words and the multiple ways that cultural groups communicate for different purposes. They have opportunities to make connections between more formal academic uses of language and social and cultural shifts around language. Explicit discussion of the varying purposes and uses of language can also call attention to the rich language resources that nonnative English speakers bring to the classroom (Gonzalez, Moll, & Amanti, 1992). Furthermore, valuing the funds of knowledge that students bring to our classes is a hallmark of culturally responsive instruction that supports students from diverse backgrounds (Gay, 2000; Ladson-Billings, 1994; Lee, 1993).

What Is Academic Language within ELA Courses?

In Chapter 1, we made a distinction between general academic vocabulary and domain-specific vocabulary. In this chapter, we explore three different kinds of academic vocabulary that students encounter within ELA courses: general academic vocabulary, general literary vocabulary (Tier Two), and domain-specific vocabulary (Tier Three). General academic vocabulary refers to terms that are not unique to a particular discipline but that reflect processes of thinking and reasoning about the world. These words might be challenging and their definitions might be difficult to glean from context, but they are often central to reading, writing, and thinking within and about complex texts. Words such as *definition, explanation, analysis,* and *conclusion* are examples of general academic vocabulary in ELA courses. These words are often used within multiple disciplines, and their meanings remain relatively constant.

Arid, circuitous, ephemeral, ostentatious, perfidy. Many an English teacher has spent hours poring over lists of SAT/ACT vocabulary, trying to identify the key words that students need to know in order to read more challenging texts and to pass the dreaded college entrance exams. This chapter offers some fun approaches to teaching these Tier Two words. We argue that while there is a place for stand-alone word study, many of these terms can be taught in the context of engaging texts from a variety of different genres and media. See, for example, one of the opening paragraphs of *The Book Thief* by Mark Zusak (2005). Words that might be challenging for students and that might require fast or focused instruction are *italicized.*

> I am in all truthfulness attempting to be cheerful about this whole topic, though most people find themselves *hindered* in believing me, no matter my *protestations.* Please, trust me. I most definitely can be cheerful. I can be *amiable.* Agreeable. *Affable.* And that's only the A's. (p. 3)

In this quote, the narrator, Death, introduces and tries to endear himself to us despite our preconceptions. Over the course of the opening pages, he continues to convince us that he is "not *malicious*" (p. 5) and that when the readers' own time comes, he will stand over us "as *genially* as possible" (p. 4). What a wonderful teaching opportunity this affords us! Students can explore these challenging vocabulary terms to construct an impression of Zusak's narrator and to generate questions about what Death's role might be in the ensuing narrative.

In ELA courses, domain-specific academic vocabulary words, often referred to as Tier Three words, allow students access to discipline-specific ways of communicating around reading and writing literary and informational texts. When teachers introduce students to the typical structure of a short story, they often introduce words such as *exposition, conflict,* and *denouement.* The first two terms, *exposition* and *conflict,* have nuanced meanings within the context of the short story. As a result, those definitions need to be taught explicitly. On the other hand, *denouement* is often unfamiliar to most students, and also needs to be taught explicitly if it will be used within the classroom conversations about the short story. These examples remind us that when we invite students to participate in the discourse of ELA, we must both refine and expand their prior knowledge of key academic vocabulary. See Figure 4.1 for additional domain-specific academic words that are frequently taught in ELA courses.

As we introduced in Chapter 2, knowledge of domain-specific vocabulary is key to helping students enter the discourse community, or the community of readers, writers, speakers and thinkers, within that particular discipline. In other words, academic vocabulary enables students to join and engage with that discourse community. Some of the words listed in Figure 4.1, such as *motif* and *hyperbo*le, are new to most students. Others, such as *conflict, rhythm,* and *point of view* seem familiar but take on unique meanings within the context of the ELA class. As these words become parts of students' receptive and expressive vocabularies, they are able to engage more fully as budding literary critics, poets, and journalists.

metaphor	simile	analogy	aphorism
characterization	genre	hyperbole	motif
theme	denouement	doppelganger	antagonist
protagonist	exposition	point of view	resolution
connotation	denotation	alliteration	free verse
iambic pentameter	rhythm	rhyme	conflict
claim	warrant	argument	thesis

FIGURE 4.1. Sample list of domain-specific academic vocabulary in ELA.

Key Understandings about Vocabulary in ELA

- Flooding the classroom with words supports both intentional and incidental word learning.
- Students deserve to see and experiment with a variety of word learning strategies.
- Focused vocabulary instruction can build background knowledge for and support close reading and comprehension of complex literary and argumentative texts.
- Students bring knowledge of language and language structures to class; instruction should capitalize on this prior knowledge.
- Vocabulary learning *can* be engaging, student driven, and fun.

CCSS Guidelines: How Are the ELA Standards Treated across Grades?

A closer look at the reading, writing, and speaking–listening strands reveal important priorities for teaching and learning academic vocabulary in ELA. Figure 4.2 illustrates the central role of academic vocabulary in the CCSS for ELA. For each strand, a sample of academic vocabulary associated with the anchor standards is presented to illustrate the kinds of words and concepts that middle and high school students will need to know and use in order to meet the CCSS requirements.

As we look across the ELA language strand, we notice that while the standards require an increasing degree of independent word learning, the core skills expected of students remain relatively constant between grades 6 and 12. Figure 4.3 on p. 54 can help you trace the progression of word-learning skills that are expected as students move from grades 6 to 12.

Flooding ELA Classrooms with Words

In Chapter 3 we presented three focal ways of conceptualizing the teacher's role in vocabulary instruction: flood, fast, and focused. English teachers are often experts at flooding their classrooms with words: bookshelves overflowing with books they've collected over the years; every spare inch of wall space covered in favorite poems, quotes, and student writings; desks piled high with student narratives charged with using vivid description or creative metaphors.

In these settings, words wash over and drift with students constantly. Sometimes, though, we need to spend a little bit more time celebrating and intentionally calling students' attention to the words around us. As Hiebert and Kamil (2005)

Category of Anchor Standards	Sample of associated academic vocabulary for students to know
Reading literature strand	
Key Ideas and Details	*details, retell, central idea, summarize*
Craft and Structure	*phrase, clause, punctuation, structure, beginning, conclusion, metaphor, drama, dialogue*
Integration of Knowledge and Ideas	*relationship, compare, contrast, mood*
Writing strand	
Text Types and Purposes	*opinion, narrative, informative, explanatory, transitional word, phrase*
Production and Distribution	*planning, revising, editing, sequence, organizational structure, concluding statement*
Speaking and listening strand	
Comprehension and Collaboration	*collaborate, explain, clarify, claim, evidence*
Presentation of Knowledge and Ideas	*report, main idea, details, fact, pace*
Language strand	
Vocabulary Acquisition and Use	*clarify, context, affixes, consult, nuances, figurative language, verify, connotations, denotations*

FIGURE 4.2. Key CCSS Anchor Standard categories for ELA and associated academic vocabulary.

remind us, "Vocabulary is not a developmental skill or one that can ever be seen as fully mastered. The expansion and elaboration of vocabularies is something that extends across a lifetime" (p. 2). Our imperative in the upper grades, then, is to figure out how we can cultivate joy, enthusiasm, and a sense of purpose for the lifelong word learning that is essential to one's continued growth. You can use the following strategies to create a classroom culture that celebrates language and helps to inspire an interest in lifelong word learning.

Read-Alouds

Reading aloud a wide range of texts is a powerful strategy for engaging students with words and for promoting both receptive and expressive word learning within the classroom. Serafini and Giorgis (2003) offer 13 reasons why teachers should consistently read aloud to older students; these include connecting students with

Grades 6–8	Grades 9–10	Grades 11–12
Determine or clarify the meaning of unknown and multiple-meaning words and phrases based on grade __ reading and content, choosing flexibly from a range of strategies. (CCSS.ELA-LITERACY.L.6-12.4)		
Use context (e.g., the overall meaning of a sentence or paragraph; a word's position or function in a sentence) as a clue to the meaning of a word or phrase. (CCSS.ELA-LITERACY.L.6-12.4.A)		
Use common, grade-appropriate Greek or Latin affixes and roots as clues to the meaning of a word (e.g., *audience, auditory, audible*).	Identify and correctly use patterns of word changes that indicate different meanings or parts of speech (e.g., *analyze, analysis, analytical; advocate, advocacy*).	Identify and correctly use patterns of word changes that indicate different meanings or parts of speech (e.g., *conceive, conception, conceivable*).
Interpret figures of speech (e.g., personification) in context.	Interpret figures of speech (e.g., euphemism, oxymoron) in context and analyze their role in the text.	Interpret figures of speech (e.g., hyperbole, paradox) in context and analyze their role in the text.
Use the relationship between particular words (e.g., cause/effect, part/whole, item/category) to better understand each of the words.	Analyze nuances in the meaning of words with similar denotations.	Analyze nuances in the meaning of words with similar denotations.
Distinguish among the connotations (associations) of words with similar denotations (definitions) (e.g., *stingy, scrimping, economical, unwasteful, thrifty*).		
Acquire and use accurately grade-appropriate general academic and domain-specific words and phrases; gather vocabulary knowledge when considering a word or phrase important to comprehension or expression.		

FIGURE 4.3. CCSS ELA Language strand across time.

new text structures and content-area concepts, providing students an opportunity for extended discussion, and introducing quality models for students' own writing.

I (Laura) often began each school year by reading Lewis Carroll's poem "Jabberwocky" aloud to my students. I introduced the poem simply by asking the students to help me figure out what was going on. As I began reading, "Twas brillig, and the slithy toves did gyre and gimble in the wabe," students began to chuckle. This always lightened the mood a bit, and it introduced students to how authors play with, explore, and reimagine language depending on their purpose. As students worked in pairs to "translate" Carroll's nonsense words into recognizable words and ultimately share their creations with the class, they were also able to explore the context clues that aid meaning-making and discuss the power of choosing "just the right word" for a particular purpose.

Read-alouds are a particularly powerful tool for ELs, whose receptive vocabulary often develops before their expressive vocabulary. A few years ago, 17-year-old Peter immigrated to Wisconsin from Liberia. Although Peter had been enrolled in school in his home country and although his native language was English, his teacher quickly realized that he struggled to read even the most common sight words. Upon her school librarian's suggestion, she introduced him to rapper Tupac Shakur's poetry anthology, *A Rose in the Concrete*. They engaged in modeled, repeated readings of Tupac's poems, and his teacher developed mini-lessons around key sounds and words within the poems. Ultimately, working in conjunction with his ESL teacher, they applied this approach with key words that Peter was encountering—or would encounter—in his sheltered English and social studies classes.

Many ELA departments and special education teachers possess audio versions of core classroom texts. By sharing snippets of these audio versions in class, teachers can help students become familiar with the style and language of the writer. Many word-processing programs, e-readers, and smartphones now come with a text-to-speech feature. Using this feature, students can have a text read aloud to them, even when they're not in the classroom. Your school library might also have additional listening devices and/or software programs that students can access.

Think-Alouds

We often use think-alouds in conjunction with read-alouds; think-alouds allow us to model word-learning strategies as we encounter unfamiliar words in complex text. For example, consider the opening lines of this high-interest article that a teacher might share with students at the start of class:

> In 1965, when Mary Beth Tinker was 13 years old, she wore a black armband to her junior high school to protest the Vietnam War. The school promptly suspended her, but her protest eventually led to a landmark Supreme Court case: *Tinker v. Des Moines*. In their verdict, the court vindicated Tinker by saying students do not "shed their constitutional rights to freedom of speech or expression at the schoolhouse gate." (Wheeler, 2014)

The teacher knows that some of the vocabulary in this text might be challenging for students, but she recognizes that the term *vindicated* is particularly important because it helps convey the outcome of the case. As a result, she might read the previous excerpt aloud and then share the following thoughts with her students:

> "I'm not sure what the word *vindicated* means. Based on where it is in the sentence and the suffix *-ed*, it looks like an action verb that describes something the court did to Tinker when it announced its ruling in her case. The quote from the court's ruling that follows helps me understand that the Supreme Court believed that the school district should not have suspended Tinker for wearing an armband. Because of this, vindicated probably means 'proved [Tinker] right' or 'agreed with.' What do you think? Does this makes sense in the context of the sentence, or do you think it means something different?"

By sharing high-interest texts regularly and by modeling effective in-context vocabulary learning strategies, teachers can simultaneously pique students' interest in text and support their independent word learning. (Kelly Gallagher posts high-interest articles weekly on his website: *www.kellygallagher.org/article-of-the-week*.) In this setting, words wash over students constantly. Sometimes, though, we need to spend a little bit more time celebrating and calling out the words around us. Sometimes, we need to make those words visible.

Word Walls

Ms. Breezee selects key words from each unit during the year; these units are organized around both key texts and themes. She introduces the words incrementally and then displays them on her classroom wall so that students can access them as they are engaged in discussion and writing activities (see Figure 4.4a).

Word walls are frequently seen in elementary schools, but more middle and secondary teachers are starting to see the benefits of making words visible throughout their classrooms (Allen, 1999). In the example above, Ms. Breezee chose to organize her word wall by units of study; others may choose to organize their word walls alphabetically or topically. For example, in preparation to teach *Night* by Elie Wiesel, Ms. Simonson must take into account the fact that students might be unfamiliar with many of the English and Yiddish words that are used to describe characters and setting within the novel. As a result, she creates two categories within her word wall: Character and Setting.

Students choose a focal word to explore, develop a visual representation of that word, and are ultimately responsible for teaching their word to the class. After this student-led instruction, Ms. Simonson asks students to place their word poster in the appropriate category on their word wall (see Figure 4.4b). As the class engages with *Night*, Ms. Simonson consistently calls attention to the words on the word wall and encourages students to use these words in both class discussion and in their written texts.

(a)

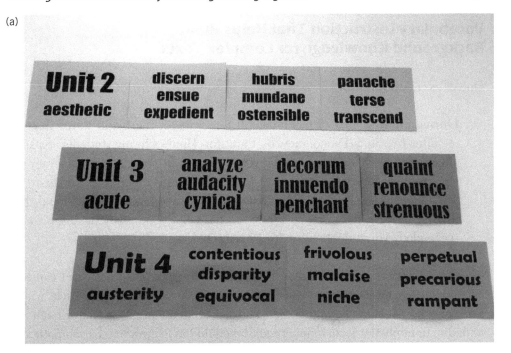

(b)

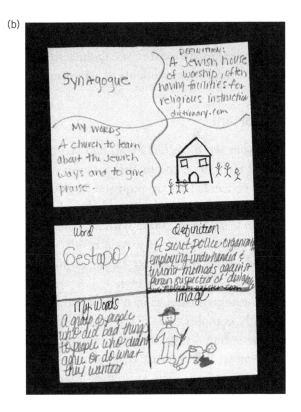

FIGURE 4.4. Sample ELA word walls.

Vocabulary Instruction That Helps Build Background Knowledge for Complex Texts

One of us (Laura) recalls:

> "During my first year of teaching, I'll never forget the blank stares that met me after I recited 'Democracy' by Langston Hughes to my students at a small alternative school on the north side of Chicago. I began again: 'Democracy will not come / Today, not this year / Nor ever / Through compromise and fear.' The questions I posed to start a discussion of the poem fell flat as well, and then, finally, it struck me. 'Can someone tell me what democracy means?' No one responded. My students were 16–20 years old."

Laura's experience highlights the impact a single conceptual word can have on students' comprehension of a text, be it a poem, an informational article, a short story or a novel. Had she anticipated that her students might not have been able to define or apply the term *democracy*, she could have introduced a semantic map or Frayer Model activity for students to complete collaboratively prior to reading the poem. Or she could have used a quick formative assessment to gauge students' understanding and provide necessary instruction before she continued with her second attempt. In this section, we explore vocabulary strategies that help build the background knowledge required for students to access complex texts.

Why Is This So Important?

Laura's students that year were students who had struggled in school for various reasons. We know that students come to our classrooms with varying experiences with the language and concepts that are required for deep understanding of course topics. Multiple studies have shown that vocabulary knowledge is a predictor of reading comprehension (e.g., Nagy, 2005); without that knowledge, students struggle to make sense of texts independently. As a result, we can't assume that if we simply assign a text and accompanying note-taking requirements for homework that students will be able to access it on their own.

In addition, the authors of the CCSS have called upon teachers to introduce students to increasingly complex texts. They also direct ELA teachers to incorporate additional informational texts into their instruction. These texts are often complex precisely because they consist of longer, less common words that are more likely to challenge students. The strategies below can be used to help students build the background knowledge that is essential to comprehending complex texts.

Pass the Page

Ms. Swenson developed a strategy called "Pass the Page" (see also "Pass the Concept" in Chapter 6) for a semester-long ELA elective called "Rising Up." In this semester-long class, 11th- and 12th-grade students explore how language (oral and written) has been used to stand up against injustice, to empower and to disempower individuals. She begins each year by listing the key course concepts—*justice, power, identity, oppression, culture,* and *language*—on the whiteboard. She knows that while most students are familiar with these words, they might not have the deep, complex, and nuanced understandings that will be essential to exploring the course topics and readings. The students receive numbers (1–6), with each number corresponding to one of the words listed. When prompted, the students write anonymously for 2 minutes about what they think their term means, what it sounds like it means, or connections they can make between the term and their own experiences. After 2 minutes, each student passes his/her page, and the next student reads the first entry and adds his or her own thoughts and connections.

After every student has contributed their ideas to each term, students are instructed to meet in groups based on the number/term they were assigned initially and read through all of the entries collectively, highlighting any commonalities or ideas that resonate with them. Based on this conversation, the group receives a blank piece of paper and is instructed to create a "poetic definition" of the word. Often, this definition takes the form of a found poem; if there are artists in the group, Ms. Swenson encourages them to add images to support their definitions. Ultimately, students share their definitions with the class, and they are posted in the class for the duration of the semester. The next day, these definitions are used as the springboard for a personal narrative writing assignment; over the course of the semester, the students consistently refer back to these poetic definitions as they refine their understandings of these key terms.

Knowledge Rating Charts

We have found Knowledge Rating Charts (Blachowicz, 1987) to be one of the most useful approaches for introducing texts that include both unfamiliar vocabulary words and unfamiliar concepts. To initiate a conversation about how online reading and searching might be affecting readers' brains, a high school English teacher wanted his students to read and discuss an article by Nicholas Carr (2008) titled, "Is Google Making Us Stupid?: What the Internet Is Doing to Our Brains." However, he recognized that both the vocabulary and the structure of the text would be challenging for many of his students. After working with a literacy coach (Laura) to explore potential scaffolds for this assignment, she developed the Knowledge Rating Chart shown in Figure 4.5.

Word, concept, or allusion	Know it well	Have heard it or seen it	No clue	Notes/Definition
malfunctioning				
neural circuitry				
online media				
Google				
efficiency				
Taylorism				
artificial intelligence				
distraction				
My PREDICTION:				

FIGURE 4.5. Sample Knowledge Rating Chart.

First, Laura shared the title of the article with students and asked them to predict what the author might discuss. After these initial predictions were recorded on the board, students were asked to rate their knowledge of the words in Figure 4.5. After finishing this step, students gathered in small groups to share their responses with each other. While the students worked in groups, the teacher and literacy coach circulated around the room, collecting data about which words seemed to be a struggle for most of the students. In this sense, the Knowledge Rating can be used as a formative assessment to help a teacher determine his/her next instructional move. Based on this quick assessment, the teacher can determine whether to review all words with the full class or to address one or two key terms that proved a challenge. In this case, the teacher knew that *Taylorism* (a reference to Frederick Taylor's scientific management principle) would require additional explanation.

As a final extension of the Knowledge Rating activity, a teacher might ask students to generate an additional prediction about the article. In the lesson described above, these predictions were recorded on a whiteboard so that they were visible to students as they read the article. Students were prompted to omit, revise, or confirm these predictions as they continued through the text.

One caveat: In order to support comprehension of the target text, the words chosen for a Knowledge Rating must be central to the author's message. This means that the teacher should not choose all words that students might struggle with; rather, the words selected should provoke a discussion of key ideas and concepts that emerge within the text.

Use vocabulary to make predictions about . . . (words may be used more than once)	
Setting *Reservation/Rez* *isolated*	**What might the setting be like?** *It might take place on an isolated Indian Reservation.*
Characters *Indians inseparable* *elder* *nomad*	**What do you think about the character(s)?** *The main characters will be Indians; a few of them might be inseparable.* *Some might be elders, and some might move a lot like nomads.*
Actions *displace* *suspended*	**What might happen?** *If a character gets suspended, he or she might be displaced and have to live somewhere else.*
Resolution	**How might it end?**
What questions do you have? *Why might someone get suspended? Will he or she have to leave the reservation?*	
Mystery words *cerebral, seizures*	

FIGURE 4.6. Prereading Vocab-O-Gram for *The Absolutely True Diary of a Part-Time Indian* by Sherman Alexie (2007).

Vocab-O-Grams

Like Vocabulary Knowledge Ratings, Vocab-O-Grams (Blachowicz & Fischer, 2010) allow students to simultaneously learn new vocabulary words and make predictions about an upcoming reading. However, Vocab-O-Grams require students to begin to categorize those words and to use them to draw inferences about various aspects of a narrative text. The Vocab-O-Gram in Figure 4.6 was completed as students prepared to read *The Absolutely True Diary of a Part-Time Indian* by Sherman Alexie (2007). Students received a list of words that described various aspects of Alexie's novel, and they organized these words using the categories provided.

Semantic Maps

Semantic maps, also known as concept maps, are a useful way for students to explore the relationships between words and to delve into a key word or topic in depth. In addition, they have shown to be more effective for student word learning than learning solely through definitions (MacKinnon, 1993). Semantic maps can be used before, during, or after reading a text to support student learning of new words and, if completed at the end of a reading or lesson, to assess students' deepening knowledge of key terms or concepts. While we discuss one form of a semantic map, a Frayer model, below, many teachers we know have adapted these maps in order to help students focus on a particularly salient feature of a word, to enable them to represent concepts pictorially, or to allow student input into structure of the model. You can find a variety of concept map templates and examples online.

A Frayer model, also sometimes referred to as a four-square, is one type of concept map that can help students categorize and refine their understanding of a key topic or concept. Frayer models allow students to identify both examples and nonexamples of a key concept; these examples and nonexamples can be drawn from students' own experiences. Figure 4.7 shows a completed Frayer model exploring the term *memoir*.

While presenting these mapping templates, we try to keep in mind Berthoff's (1981) caveat about schematic organizers: such devices can be overly emphasized to the extent that we lose sight of their larger purpose (p. 76). Because of this, it is imperative that teachers are choosing—or creating—vocabulary templates that allow the precise kind of word learning that is appropriate for a given instructional context or purpose. Many different versions of concept and semantic maps can be found online that can be adapted to specific instructional needs. In addition, teachers should make these instructional purposes known to students so they too can see why, for example, refining their understanding of what a memoir is—and is not—is necessary for an upcoming activity.

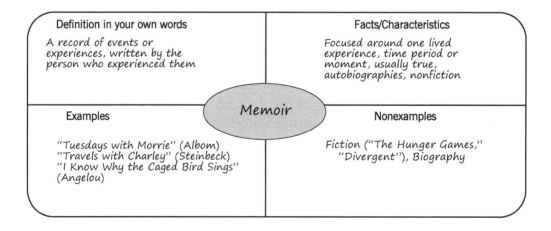

FIGURE 4.7. Sample Frayer model for *memoir*.

Vocabulary Instruction That Supports Comprehension *during* the Reading Process

When students enter middle and high school, much of their reading occurs outside of the school. Whether they're reading for pleasure or for homework, they are going to encounter multiple unfamiliar words. As a result, they need multiple strategies that they can use flexibly in order to meet the demands of a particular text or language context. We recommend that students ask the following questions when they encounter an unfamiliar word during their reading.

1. "Does not knowing this word prevent me from understanding the sentence?"
2. "If not, keep reading."
3. "If yes, ask the following questions: 'Do any of the parts of this word look familiar?' 'Do I recognize any roots, affixes or suffixes?' 'Do I know variants of this word?' 'Cognates?' 'Does this help me?'"
4. "Are there any context clues that can help me get the gist of what the word means?"
5. "Do I need to ask someone? Consult a dictionary? Look it up on my phone? Ask Siri?"
6. "How much do I need to know about this? Am I going to see it word again? If so, where can I write down the definition so that I remember it? On the page? In a word journal?"

We consider the questions above as a starting place for teachers. After initial teacher-led instruction and modeling of vocabulary learning strategies, teachers may choose to develop these questions collaboratively with students. This activity requires students to engage metacognitively with their own learning and articulate the strategies that have been most effective for them. Below, we've detailed a few strategies that can be modeled to support in-context, independent word learning.

Using Context Clues

Consider the first line from Eudora Welty's (1982) short story "Circe," which reimagines Odysseus's meeting with Circe from alternative perspective.

> Needle in the air, I stopped what I was making. From the upper *casement*, my lookout on the sea, I saw them *disembark* and find the path; I heard that whole drove of mine break loose on the beautiful strangers. (p. 531)

Students familiar with Homer's *Odyssey* might recognize this scene as Circe describes it: the moment when Odysseus and his crew land on Aeaea, Circe's island. However, they might need to use context clues such as *upper* and *lookout on the sea*, coupled with a quick dictionary search, to determine that *casement* refers to some kind of a high room with a window. A quick dictionary search can allow students to further refine that definition: *casement* is, in fact, a window that hinges open like a door.

Students might also use within-word context clues to help them determine the meaning of *disembark*. They might recognize the prefix *dis* from more familiar words like *dislike*, and *disprove*, and they might know that it typically negates or indicates the opposite of the root it is attached to. A teacher might then ask students: "If *embark* means to board a ship or an aircraft, what might the term *disembark* mean in this context?" Students familiar with the epic poem will relate this to the ships that have transported Odysseus and his crew on their adventures. Knowing the title of this piece, they will be able to deduce that Circe is recounting the moment when Odysseus and his crew arrive on her island. In order to make this inference, students must have some familiarity with common morphemes (roots, suffixes, prefixes). We explore the potential of morphemic awareness in more detail in the section below.

To explore "in-context" definitions, we recommend *Thefreedictionary.com*. This website offers definitions of words from multiple sources, including references made to the word in classic literature. For example, when searching for the meaning of *malicious*, definitions from three different dictionaries appear, as does a thesaurus entry and three different references to the word in classic texts. One of these references is from Jack London's book *Before Adam*: "And I quickly learned to be afraid of him and his **malicious** pranks." By clicking the link "View in Context" that appears after each quote, one can see the full transcript of the original text, with the target word highlighted.

Morphemic Awareness: Creating Independent Word Learners

Imagine that you read the following sentence in an online news article: *The German soccer team arrived back home to a euphony of cheers, well-wishes, and celebratory songs after winning the 2014 FIFA World Cup.* You might not have used the word *euphony* before, but you draw on multiple strategies to help you figure it out. First, you draw on your prior knowledge of the German team's win and assume that returning home would be a joyous, celebrated event. If you didn't know this at the start, the final adverb phrase alerts you to this background information. Next, you might notice the context clues embedded within the sentence itself: "cheers", "well-wishes", "celebratory songs" all connote sounds that would be pleasing to a winning team. But if you recognized the morphemes *eu* (good) and *phon* (sound), you would have grasped the general meaning of the word immediately.

Morphemes

Morphemes are the smallest units within a word that serve a grammatical purpose and impact meaning. Roots, suffixes, and prefixes are all examples of morphemes that readers use to help them identify unfamiliar terms they encounter. Carlisle (1995) found that readers vary in their "conscious awareness of the morphemic structures of words and their ability to reflect on and manipulate that structure" (p. 194, as cited in Goodwin, Gilbert, & Cho, 2013). As teachers, we can help students increase their familiarity with and awareness of these morphemes and model how we use morphemes to help us determine the meaning of unfamiliar words.

As students learn to identify these "clues within words," they are more likely to be able to read (Goodwin et al., 2013) and determine the meaning of unfamiliar words (Kieffer & Lesaux, 2007; McCutcheon, Green, & Abbott, 2008; Rasinski, Padak, Newton, & Newton, 2011). As a result, teachers might use the list of common affixes (suffixes and prefixes) in Figure 4.8 as a guide when they plan their instruction. Baumann and Graves (2010) suggest organizing instruction around affix "families," or affixes that have similar meanings; this way, students have access to multiple morphemes simultaneously. In addition, students can generate a web of words that all contain the same affix. If a full-school approach to vocabulary instruction exists, teachers can explore how similar affixes appear within their disciplines.

ELs are often particularly adept at recognizing morphemes; depending on the word's etymologic origin, students might recognize elements of their first language within these unfamiliar words (e.g., *abstain—abstenerse*). Articulating these connections can help support ELs' word learning and can support their classroom participation. In Figure 4.9, we've listed a sample of Spanish cognates that a teacher might reference during ELA instruction. A full list of Spanish cognates, organized by subject area, can be found at *http://spanishcognates.org*.

Vocabulary Instruction That Supports the Writing Process: Strategies for Integrating New Words into Student Writing

To help develop students' word consciousness (Blachowicz & Fisher, 2014), teachers serve as mentors and role models. There is much written about the use of mentor texts (both published and teacher generated) to support writing instruction for adolescents (see Gallagher, 2011); mentor texts can be especially powerful as teachers help students develop a careful, deliberate attention to the word choices they make within their own writing. The teaching ideas that follow both use and probe mentor texts in order to help students focus their attention on the deliberate word choices authors make.

Affix	Meaning	Example
Prefixes		
co-	with, together	*cooperate, coordinate coworker*
dis-	not, opposite from	*disagree, dishonest, disappear*
em-, en-	in, to put into	*embed, encourage*
ex-	former, out	*ex-husband, export, excavate*
in-, im-, ir-	not	*inaccurate, imbalance, irregular*
inter-	among, between	*international, intercession*
non-	not	*nonviolent, nonfiction, nontoxic*
over-	too much	*overbearing, overpriced, overeat*
pre-	before	*precaution, prewar*
pro-	favor	*pro-education, pro-environment*
re-	again, back	*replay, redo, revision*
super-	over, more than usual	*superstar, superpower, supernova*
trans-	across	*transatlantic, transport*
un-	not	*unhappy, unfamiliar*
Suffixes		
-al	relating to	*optical, natural, nautical*
-ble	inclined to	*sociable, perishable, divisible*
-ence, -ance, -ancy	quality of, state of	*difference, prominence, infancy*
-er, -or	one who does something	*teacher, sculptor, creditor*
-ful	full of	*joyful, careful*
-ian	relating to, someone who engages in	*mathematician, musician*
-less	without	*fearless, hopeless*
-ly	in the manner of	*gingerly, figuratively, happily*
-ment	act or process of, result of	*government, fulfillment*
-ness	state or quality of being	*darkness, sadness*
-tion, -sion	state, quality, or act of	*saturation, division*
-ty, -ity	state or quality of	*loyalty, honesty, humidity*

FIGURE 4.8. Alphabetical list of common affixes and their meanings. For a list of common affixes organized by affix "family," see Baumann et al. (2007).

English	Spanish
abbreviation	*abbreviación*
conflict	*conflicto*
compare	*comprare*
conjunction	*conjunción*
literature	*literatura*
modify	*modificar*
scene	*escena*
theme	*tema*

FIGURE 4.9. Examples of common ELA-focused Spanish cognates.

Becoming a Collector of Words

When our classrooms become laboratories for words—places where students can experiment with words and word usage, can try on new words to see how they fit—students begin to naturally seek out and adopt new words into their lives and personal vocabularies.
—THOMAS B. SMITH (2008, p. 22)

Many middle and high school teachers we work with ask their students to maintain personalized vocabulary journals that, in effect, become "laboratories for words." While these journals have different names (Word Learning journals, Vocabulary Journals, etc.) and are maintained in different media (notebook, class wiki, online), they are spaces where students can record both words presented in class and "Golden Words" they happen upon in their class readings or in their independent reading.

Ms. Simonson views these journals as spaces where students can truly gain ownership over the words that they study. She uses that term *ownership* often when talking to students about their word learning, and she requires students to include metacognitive reflections on their vocabulary learning. In their journals, students are asked to respond to questions such as "Which words do you feel like you own and how do you know?"; "What's working for you?"; "What's not working?"; "How can I help you gain ownership over the new words you're learning?" Ms Simonson revealed, "I'm more concerned about students having ownership of the words . . . growth is the most important aspect of vocabulary development." Because of this, the journals become places where student artists can draw graphic representations of word, where poets can create found poems, where budding architects can create new sophisticated semantic maps to help them draw connections between the old and the new. They also become rich sources of information for their teacher, who can use them to assess student progress and to dialogue with students about their learning.

Vocabulary Hunts

Early in the year, Ms. Simonson introduces her 12th-grade English students to the notion that all words are *not* equal; authors choose words deliberately, and the specific words they choose have a powerful impact on how a reader interacts with their text. To explore this idea, her students search for "golden words or phrases" in the literature that they read; Scott, Skobel, and Wells (2008) termed a similar instructional approach "Gifts of Words." These words, Simonson explains, should be ones that resonate with students as they read; she intentionally leaves the instructions open ended. Students record these words in their vocabulary notebooks, and they note the context in which they appeared in the text. The following day, students gather in small groups and share their "golden words or phrases" with their peers, explaining why they think the author chose that particular word or phrase over other choices. The group selects one or two words or phrases to share with the entire class. Finally, each student completes an entry in their vocabulary journals in which they share their reflections about the words and phrases that were chosen and about their impacts on a given text.

Often, Ms. Simonson will prompt students by asking, "Do you think that was the first word that came to the author's mind as he/she wrote this?" In doing so, she opens the door to conversations about the intentional use and refinement of language that authors engage in constantly. She explained that this activity has a direct impact on the students' own writing. It heightens their awareness of the power and connotations of words, and they become more selective about the words they choose as they craft their own texts in her class.

Scott et al. (2008) note that the "Gifts of Words" approach supports students' understanding of how writers craft their own texts. In essence, students learn how to "read like writers" as they begin to view their selected words and phrases as mentor texts (Gallagher, 2011; Ray, 1999) that they can draw upon for their own writing. Historically, these collections of interesting quotes or passages are called commonplace books. Harvard University has a unique collection of commonplace books from the 17th, 18th, and 19th centuries, some of which can be viewed online at *http://ocp.hul.harvard.edu/reading/commonplace.html*.

The Power and Possibilities of Word Choice: Exploring the "What Ifs?"

Homing in on author's word choice can help support the close reading that allows students to critically analyze an author's perspective and purpose. As early as grade 6, the CCSS Reading Literature and Informational Text grade-level standards place particular emphasis on students' ability to "analyze the impact of a specific word choice on meaning and tone." By the end of 10th grade, students are expected to "analyze the cumulative impact" that an author's word choice has on an entire text.

Consider the opening lines of Robert Frost's iconic poem "The Road Not Taken": "Two roads diverged in a yellow wood." How might one's interpretation of the poem change if Frost had used the word *split* or *separated* instead of *diverged* in the opening line of the poem? What connotations does the word *diverge* have? What tone does it reveal? What mood does it evoke in the reader? By asking students to explore the impact that a particular word—and potential alternatives—has on a piece of text, teachers can draw students' attention to the particular choices that writers make and the effect those choices have on the reader.

Signal Words

Authors skillfully select words that alert their readers to changes in time, character, narration, ideas, and so forth. When incorporating quotations, the signal words authors choose fulfill multiple functions. In literary fiction or nonfiction works, writers use signal words to introduce a quote, to establish the mood and purpose of the quote, and to highlight key details about who is speaking. Consider the following sentences. What assumptions can you make about Brenda and about the situation based on each sentence?

> Brenda bellowed, "Don't put the vase there. It might break!"
> Brenda suggested, "Don't put the vase there. It might break."

Encourage students to use the above examples as models as they work in pairs to experiment with using powerful signal words in their own writing.

Within informational texts, signal words introduce the relationship between the main text and a quotation, they also indicate the author's relationship to the ideas he/she is writing about and the relationship between ideas within a single text. As increasingly complex texts are introduced to students, it becomes even more imperative to call students' attention to these signal words and the ways in which they can support reading comprehension and increase the clarity in the students' own writing. The web in Figure 4.10 depicts just a few examples of the many signal words that authors use as they craft informational or argumentative texts.

Interactive Vocabulary Work: Making Vocabulary Learning a Social, Collaborative, and Fun Process

Word-rich classrooms involve students in word puzzles, games, riddles, and rhymes; making these activities and resources accessible to students supports their word learning (Blachowicz & Fisher, 2004). Sometimes, learning words can be downright fun and can bring students together to engage in creative work. While many of

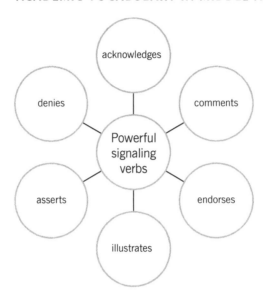

FIGURE 4.10. Signal words web: Informational text.

the strategies we've shared thus far can be completed collaboratively, the strategies below require collaboration and a bit of creativity.

Vocabulary Charades

Ms. Simonson incorporates kinesthetic learning experiences in her vocabulary work with her students. With a partner, students are asked to physically represent a key word from one of the texts they are studying as a class. Because different pairs choose to represent that word differently, the class then engages in a discussion about which representation most fully and accurately reflects the word's meaning. After the class reaches a consensus, students record that word in their vocabulary journals, including any graphic or written clues that will help them remember the word in the future. Ms. Simonson often uses this activity when she needs to pre-teach vocabulary to support comprehension of a challenging text. In this case, she explores an online dictionary together with the students and helps them select the definition that best fits the meaning of the target word in the upcoming text. When using vocab charades as a vocabulary review activity, no definitions are required.

Vocabulary Instruction for Speaking and Listening

Walk into a middle or high school ELA class, and you will often be in the midst of a rich debate about right and wrong, about the morality of characters' actions, about the applicability of a text's themes to the "real world." These conversations provide fertile ground for both incidental and focused vocabulary instruction. They often give students multiple exposures to target words, supporting the continued development of their receptive vocabularies. Simple reminders to use words from the class word wall or unit vocab list, to listen to the way others frame their arguments and to use textual evidence to support one's argument can support the development of students' expressive vocabulary; these reminders can also enhance students' understanding of the language they can use to develop or refute arguments within their own writing.

Everyday Encounters

Word play can require students to activate and explore deeper understandings of key course concepts. Consider staging conversations, debates, or even speed dating sessions between two abstract or conceptual words that are central to the topic or text being studied. The teacher can provide as much or as little context for this meeting as they would like; the RAFT strategy (Santa, Havens, & Valdes, 2004) provides a template that teachers and students can work with to establish roles and contexts for these conversations or "encounters." RAFT was designed to support student writers in their consideration of the writer's purpose and audience; in our example below, you'll see that we have adapted this strategy slightly to support student conversation.

> **Role:** Fate
> **Audience:** Free Will
> **Format:** Speed Dating
> **Topic/Discussion Starter:** Why would someone want to spend time with you?

By personifying these conceptually rich words, students need to fully delve into their meanings, evaluate how they would function in different contexts, and express their understandings creatively. These conversations can also be a powerful springboard to writing assignments that require students to grapple with more complex concepts.

Individual and Group Presentations

In the book *The Skin We Speak: Thoughts on Language and Culture in the Classroom* (Baker, 2008), high school English teacher Judith Baker beautifully describes the way that her students, when allowed to explore and present about topics that interest them, learn and use the specialized language of those subject areas. She offers powerful examples of linguistically diverse students, who are sometimes reticent to speak using what Baker terms "professional" language, but who demonstrate a strong command of specialized academic language when given the formal opportunity to research and share one of their interests or passions with the class. About one student, she writes: "Kai's terminology and explanations were very precise and formal, but as with the other presentations, the class members seemed to welcome this type of language and accepted it entirely as different from ordinary class discussion" (p. 60). Subsequently, tapping into students' interests and allowing them to engage, both orally and in writing, with the technical terms associated with their interests provides authentic opportunities for students to develop their expressive domain-specific vocabularies.

Vocabulary Instruction That Supports Critical Literacy

Educators who embrace critical literacy instruction explore the ways in which language usage reflects the cultural, social, and power dynamics that exist around us. They offer students opportunities to explore how language and individual words have been used throughout history to empower some and to disempower others (Gee, 2010; Janks, 2010).

Exploring Etymologies: Becoming a Word Historian

ELA teachers often explore the ways in which language has changed in response to cultural shifts, historical events, and changing populations. A simple Google search for the phrase *English words whose meanings have changed over time* returned far more hits than we could review for this book. While we recognize that many of these sites might not be relevant, accurate, or of interest to middle and high school students, we did find a few articles, blogs, and sites that are easy to access and offer lists of words that could serve as a starting place for students:

> *http://motivatedgrammar.wordpress.com/2010/01/28/some-words-whose-meanings-have-changed-without-controversy*
> *www.dailykos.com/story/2009/05/31/735843/-The-Mad-Logophile-Words-That-Have-Changed-Their-Meaning-Part-1#*

When students have an opportunity to explore the shift that has occurred in the English language over time, they begin to understand the impact of culture, political, and social events and preferences on language usage. One of the ways that ELA teachers can inspire this interest in language shifts is by introducing students to the thousands of new words that have been introduced into our vernacular by various authors—and by their own generation.

Having Fun with Neologisms

While teaching Shakespeare, many English teachers spend time exploring the new, unique words that Shakespeare introduced within his plays. He coined many new terms simply by turning verbs into nouns (*scuffle*), combining individual words (*eyeball, eventful*), and by adding novel prefixes and suffixes where they didn't previously exist (*invincible*).

Students often don't recognize, however, that neologisms are always making their way into our written and oral communications. In fact, teenagers have often coined new words that weave their way into the popular discourse. Case in point: In June of 2014, the *Oxford English Dictionary* added more than 500 new words, including *selfie* (n), *upcycle* (v), and *eye-roll* (n). In a short video you can share with your students, staff from the *Oxford English Dictionary* describe how new words are added to the iconic dictionary (*www.youtube.com/watch?v=omoe_RMBdx4&i ndex=13&list=PL07253E5BE6882EC9*).

By giving students opportunities to explore and research the new words being added to our vernacular each day, teachers can inspire a critical conversation about what these words reveal about our political, social, and cultural preferences, technological innovations, cultural and social shifts, and so on.

Using Dynamic/Formative Assessment to Inform Instruction

When discussing many of the instructional strategies within this chapter, we mentioned that they could be used not only to introduce new words, but also as formative assessment tools. In this role, they allow teachers to assess students' word learning progress and adapt and individualize their instruction accordingly. Below, we've included some additional ideas about how word-learning strategies can be used as formative assessment tools in the ELA classroom.

• Use knowledge rating charts and student self-assessment to determine which words require instruction prior to reading.

• Collect students' records of their interactions with words in order to gauge what they are learning about specific words. Before collecting these artifacts, ask students to record one or two new strategies or tools they used to help them learn unfamiliar words.

• Have students create a word map early in a unit of study, then revisit and flesh out the map midway through and at the end of the unit. These work samples provide data on word learning over time and suggest direction for increased word study. At the end of the unit, ask students to either discuss or write a short analysis of how their understanding of that key word has changed or deepened. If the focal word reflects a key understanding of the unit, then this assessment will also allow you to assess content learning.

- Listen, listen, listen. Observe, observe, observe. Pay careful attention to your students' word choices in conversation and writing, noticing use of the words that have been taught. Since word learning is incremental, students will often misuse a new word before using it correctly, and these misuses are cause for celebration (students are trying out new words and working toward making them their own) and rich sources of information.

Vocabulary Learning Is Everyone's Responsibility

Readers who have taught interdisciplinary courses understand the possibilities that open up when (1) you have a larger block of time to work with and (2) you explore how words are used across and between disciplines. Interdisciplinary courses open up new ways of conceiving of and exploring language in multiple contexts. Students are able to explore how texts situated within different genres support and instruct each other.

For 5 years, I (Laura) collaborated with a social studies teacher on a ninth-grade English history course. During their study of the history and literature of South Africa, students explored the history and impact of apartheid on South Africa's people, economy, and culture. Together, the class read and analyzed the short story "Afrika Road" by Don Mattera (1998). In this beautifully rendered piece, the personified "Afrika Road" is the narrator; as such, it recounts the horrific violence that it has witnessed during the struggle over apartheid rule. Weaving together the disciplines allowed students to explore the complex notion of apartheid through many different text genres; Laura experienced first-hand the ways in which inter-disciplinary instruction allowed for rich exploration of challenging course terms and concepts.

One of the most exciting components of the CCSS is that it asserts that all teachers need to introduce students to the unique language considerations of their disciplines. As a result, collaboration within a school, or even between schools, around vocabulary learning can be a rich source of new ideas. We sometimes forget that foreign language teachers are fabulous resources for English teachers; they are required to be experts in vocabulary and language instruction, and they have honed their strategies over the years. As you'll see in the upcoming chapters, biology teachers have often developed effective strategies for teaching the hundreds of new words that are central to understanding their discipline. Social studies teachers understand the importance of scaffolding deep, conceptual understandings of key disciplinary terms. By collaborating with one another, teachers both within and across disciplines can support each other as they promote both intentional and incidental word learning within their classes.

Concluding Thoughts

Words—so innocent and powerless as they are, as standing
in a dictionary, how potent for good and evil they become,
in the hands of one who knows how to combine them.
      —NATHANIEL HAWTHORNE

As Hawthorne suggests above, words are imbued with power and possibility. ELA teachers, particularly in the upper grades, have the unique opportunity to introduce students to the ways in which words can be used to both empower and disempower individuals or groups (Gee, 2011; Janks, 2010). In 1972, Paolo Freire wrote about the intimate connection between reading the word and reading the world. Learning to read and write, he wrote, was about much more than simply decoding words and putting words on paper; it was about helping us understand our place in the world. Steven Stahl goes so far as to assert, "The words we know define who we are" (2005, p. 96). ELA teachers have the unique opportunity to instruct students in the intricacies of language use and to help students embrace the power "just the right word" can have in multiple contexts.

CHAPTER 5

Teaching Academic Vocabulary in History/Social Studies

This is a good time for teachers of social sciences (history, social studies, geography, and economics) to take a new look at the importance of academic vocabulary as a key to students' learning and also to think about how vocabulary can most successfully be introduced and highlighted during instruction. This attention has been stimulated by the adoption of the CCSS and the variations of those standards being constructed within particular states. The motivation behind these standards comes, at least in part, from the nearly 2-year gap in reading levels between what students are asked to read in high school and what they encounter in college and careers. To close that gap the CCSS emphasizes the importance of a cross-curricular responsibility for developing students' academic vocabularies and their ability to comprehend more challenging texts than most of those now used in secondary schools. The design of the CCSS includes ELA teachers working together with the history/social studies, science, and technical subjects teachers to develop the literacy and thinking required of college and careers.

Most history/social studies teachers don't focus instructional planning by thinking of what vocabulary to teach, but they definitely think of teaching and developing students' conceptual understanding. The concepts at the heart of the disciplines are generally represented by vocabulary that is new or minimally familiar to students. Thinking about vocabulary is just another lens through which to consider the important academic or domain-specific vocabulary. Much of the content is contained in key terms that students need to internalize. Researchers have demonstrated that understanding academic terms accounts for 80% of successful content reading (Nagy & Scott, 2000; Pressley & Allington, 2014).

Other data encourage a careful reflection on the importance of greater attention to vocabulary, too. Both the National Assessment of Educational Progress

(NAEP) results in social studies from the 2010 administration (National Center for Educational Statistics, 2010) and the recent Programme for International Student Achievement (PISA, 2012) test of financial literacy have indicated that students are not learning what the test-makers expect. On the NAEP students have shown little improvement over the last several administrations (1994, 2001, 2006, and 2010); the scores for 4th and 12th graders are flat and reflect a lack of change in students' achievement. In addition, only 45% of 12th graders scored at or above Basic on the 2010 assessment. This reality in the face of increasing expectations for learning provides added incentive for educators to think of ways to help students achieve more success in learning social studies.

The need for careful attention to the demands of the academic language and new concepts students must learn is even more important for teachers, too, because of the increasing numbers of ELs who are now in our classrooms. In fact, 2014 is the first year there are more non-Caucasian students in our schools than the traditional majority teachers have been most prepared to teach. Many of these are immigrant students who come to secondary schools with little foundation in English, and with even less knowledge of the academic discourse required for their successful participation in schooling. In their guide for teaching English language learners using the SIOP Model, Echevarria et al. (2013) explore why students have difficulty meeting teacher expectations, and why they fail to reach proficiency on the NAEP assessments. They conclude that "although history can be framed in a story-like context, students won't understand the stories if they don't know the words and they can't make connections to themselves, to other texts, or to their world. Language plays a large and important role in learning social studies, history, civics, government and economics" (p. 3). Particularly to help ELs and other, often low-income, students with limited academic vocabulary access academic English as rapidly and confidently as possible it is important to take seriously what faculty can do to support their language learning; these students need both general academic language and the domain-specific terms and ways of representing content.

The rest of this chapter is organized to help history/social studies faculty think about components of an exemplary program of support for students' vocabulary learning. Many examples of the kinds of activities middle and high school history/ social studies teachers have developed are included. The first section focuses on building a common approach across departments so students develop a consistent approach to vocabulary learning and rehearsal. Then we explain several ways history/social studies teachers can informally assess students' vocabulary knowledge. The next sections provide suggestions for classroom activities to reinforce and deepen students' understanding of concepts and how they evolve. The final section of the chapter looks at important general academic terms that students need to be able to use well in completing classroom assignments and high-stakes assessments.

Developing a Collaborative Approach to Vocabulary Learning

For all students, including ELs, to learn the many important concepts they need, it is important that they have a good grounding in understanding how to identify important terms, how to determine their meanings, and how to elaborate and expand on initial understanding as they learn more about the concepts (Nagy & Townsend, 2012; Ogle, Klemp, & McBride, 2007). These skills and habits are essential to learning vocabulary and can be monitored and reinforced by social studies teachers. They are skills and habits that should also be taught and reinforced across the disciplines and across all years of secondary schooling.

A starting place for examining what students learn about vocabulary is to have a discussion with the ELA faculty to learn how they approach vocabulary instruction. (See Chapter 4 for further elaboration of these ideas.) Ask the teachers about how they introduce and develop students skills in:

- Identifying new and important terms.
- Using context to determine how the term/s are used in the particular section of a text.
- Applying knowledge of morphology and word structure.
- Confirming or checking the meaning in other references (glossary, dictionary, other knowledgeable students/teachers).

You may also want to know what resources students have used in their vocabulary journey. Is there a module on Greek and Latin word parts that they study at some point? Have they become familiar with using morphology and word structures to help them analyze words? What expectations are there in the writing components of their courses that deal with vocabulary usage? Do students keep a vocabulary notebook?

Having a more formal discussion with a wider range of colleagues in other departments (English, world languages, ESL, and science, in particular) about specific tools and guides they want students to use to increase their knowledge and use of vocabulary learning strategies can also be productive. This important area may have been getting short shrift, and your inquiry might help everyone by developing a joint commitment and approach to vocabulary learning (Ogle & Lang, 2011). This is also a valuable discussion with the shift in the SAT from its earlier use of very esoteric vocabulary to what David Coleman, president of the College Board, has explained as assessment of highly usable words: "The changes are extensive: The SAT's rarefied vocabulary challenges will be replaced by words that are common in college courses, like 'empirical' and 'synthesis'" (Lewin, 2014, p. A1).

The more students are encouraged to approach learning new terms in consistent ways and hear the same language used across the courses they take the more likely they are to internalize and use the guides that have been provided. For example, could students be asked to expand the vocabulary notebooks they use in English for use in other subjects, specifically history? Can all history/social studies teachers guide students to monitor their attention to new vocabulary and to ask themselves, "Does this seem like an important word that I need in order to understand the meaning of this section?" If so, then they can ask, "What support does the author provide to help me understand what it means in this context?"

It is also important to learn what tools students have at their disposal for checking on the meanings of terms. Most textbooks have a consistent way of highlighting important terms for students and include glossaries for further reference. In social studies, as in science, the visual and graphic displays are often major sources of information about important concepts. Because this is very different from how words are explained in English novels and texts, it is worth explaining how these visual and graphic components support the elaboration of new content. Teachers need to ensure that students are aware of these supports for meaning and use them as they expand their understanding of the concepts being learned. In addition, teachers need to assess:

- Are there dictionaries in the classrooms?
- Do students have online dictionaries available?
- Have students learned to use the glossaries in their textbooks?
- What additional resources are available to help students learn key concepts? For instance, are there video clips and DVDs available?
- Are some of the text materials available for students to listen to?

Many free online dictionaries are available; one of these, *visuwords.com*, not only defines terms, but also graphically displays the relationships between target words and other related words.

The authors of this text are deeply involved with ways to help students increase their word power. No matter what content they study, it helps if students have an approach to unfamiliar words. We recommend that students learn to ask the following questions when they encounter unfamiliar words during their reading. (See also Chapter 4, p. 63, where this series of questions is explained.)

1. "Does not knowing this word prevent me from understanding the sentence?"
2. "If not, keep reading."
3. "If yes, ask the following questions: 'Do any of the parts of this word look

familiar?' 'Do I recognize any roots, prefixes, or suffixes?' 'Do I know variants of this word?' 'Does this help me?'"

4. "Are there any context clues that can give me the gist of what the word means?"
5. "Do the visual and graphic displays help clarify the meaning? [specific to social studies and science]?"
6. "Is the word in the glossary?"
7. "Do I need to ask someone? Consult a dictionary? Look it up on my phone? Ask Siri?"
8. "Am I going to see this word again? If so, where can I write down the definition so that I remember it? On the page? In a word journal?"

An option to teaching students the series of questions listed above is to have students and teachers develop these or a similar set of metacognitive questions collaboratively. The more students can think about their own possible ways of identifying words they need to learn the more they assume ownership of their learning. With this discussion and assessment of the school's orientation to vocabulary learning, it is possible to develop a more schoolwide approach that will help students across the years. The more teachers can collaborate in helping students become savvy about vocabulary learning, the stronger the students will become in monitoring and enjoying their own vocabulary growth. Within every department it is also valuable for faculty to check how they model interest in and approaches to learning the ever-expanding array of terms introduced to students. For example, when teachers read orally from news articles or other special texts they can make a point of pausing when reading a less or unfamiliar term, comment on the fact that this word is unusual or new, and then "think aloud" about how one can begin to build a meaning for it from context, structure, and/or visual supports.

Attention to vocabulary development and making it an enjoyable part of school life is important; teachers are key models in creating this attitude. It is also important that disciplinary teachers reinforce the vocabulary tools that students learn in ELA classes and build the connections clearly for students so they understand the word analysis strategies they know are important to use wherever they encounter unfamiliar and potentially important terms. The list of questions students can ask of unfamiliar terms they encounter is a good starting point for this collaboration and support of students. The CCSS have a clear outline of those strategies students should be using in the Language Standards strand on Vocabulary Acquisition and Use that is very similar. Studying these standards can provide another tool for shared reflection and planning.

Language Standard 4 for students in eighth grade provides the following description of what students need to do:

4. Determine or clarify the meaning of unknown and multiple-meaning words or phrases based on *grade 8 reading and content*, choosing flexibly from a range of strategies.
   a. Use context (e.g., the overall meaning of a sentence or paragraph; a word's position or function in a sentence) as a clue to the meaning of a word or phrase.
   b. Use common, grade-appropriate Greek or Latin affixes and roots as clues to the meaning of a word (e.g., *precede, recede, secede*).
   c. Consult general and specialized reference materials (e.g., dictionaries, glossaries, thesauruses), both print and digital, to find the pronunciation of a word or determine or clarify its precise meaning or its part of speech.
   d. Verify the preliminary determination of the meaning of a word or phrase (e.g., by checking the inferred meaning in context or in a dictionary). (NGA & CCSSO, 2010a, p. 53)

In addition, the CCSS Reading Standards for ELA and Literacy in History/ Social Studies, Science, and Technical Subjects includes expectations for a central focus on vocabulary. See the Craft and Structure Standard 4 in Figure 5.1.

Opportunity to explore and build ways to understand and remember unfamiliar terms comes quite regularly and naturally within social studies when primary source documents are being read and analyzed; many of these use obscure and archaic terms and are often written at a level of sophistication beyond that of most students. It is helpful that students develop comfort with managing the sometimes confusing and archaic or at least different language used in older documents. For example, even the title and introduction to the Federalist No. 10 by James Madison deserve some shared thinking: "The Utility of the Union as a Safeguard against Domestic Faction and Insurrection." Teachers who introduce this document with a "close read" (using the language of the CCSS) can help students unravel what is meant by "a well constructed Union," and "none deserves to be more accurately

Grades 6–8	Grades 9–10	Grades 11–12
Determine the meaning of words and phrases as they are used in a text, including vocabulary specific to domains related to history/social studies.	Determine the meanings of words and phrases as they are used in a text, including vocabulary describing political, social, or economic aspects of history/social studies.	Determine the meanings of words and phrases as they are used in a text, including analyzing how an author uses and refines the meaning of a key term over the course of a text (e.g., how Madison defines faction in Federalist No. 10).

FIGURE 5.1. CCSS Reading Standards for ELA and Literacy in History/Social Studies, Science, and Technical Subjects: Craft and Structure Standard 4—Central focus on vocabulary.

developed than its tendency to break and control the violence of faction." By pausing over each of the phrases and reminding students of the context and development of the argument, students can hear how an "expert" approaches such texts. Thinking aloud about the language chosen and asking questions about "violence of faction" and other concepts sets students on the right path for further reading and reflecting.

Formative Assessments

Teachers also do well to assess their own students' applications of what they have been taught about learning words. Because there is often not a good transmittal of information on what students' vocabulary proficiency and strategy knowledge is across departments and schools, teachers can learn about their students early in the term by administering some short, targeted assessments. Three easily developed and administered assessments are described below to help teachers identify how students use context, semantic knowledge, and morphology when being introduced to the vocabulary of a particular unit of study.

Use the Context

Create a series of short passages that include important domain-specific terms that are explained within the passage. Students are to underline the words, phrases, and examples that define the highlighted term. Then they write a definition for the term based on what they have read. Teachers can highlight for students the different sources of information that may be provided for their help: definitions and restatement, examples, comparisons, contrasts, and cause and effect (*therefore, as a result of . . .*) and visual images or diagrams. Most history textbooks are careful to define the targeted vocabulary and generally follow a consistent format, but students don't always avail themselves of these restatements and examples. The examples of terms in Figure 5.2 have been taken from varied levels of sources, not from one unit.

Rate Your Knowledge

This simple-to-administer pretest of students' familiarity with the important concepts involves students as well as the teacher in assessing their depth of knowledge of the important terms. The teacher creates a list of the important words and students then rate their familiarity with them on a matrix that permits them to indicate whether they know each well, have seen and are somewhat aware of its meaning, or are unfamiliar with the term (see Figure 5.3). If students indicate they know the term well, they then monitor their assessment by writing a definition or creating an image of the word. This Knowledge Rating (Blachowicz, 1987) can be

Speculation: Purchasers studied the newspaper and noted the Golden Yogurt Corporation stock had gone up 9 points in the last week. They bought shares of its stock without even knowing anything about the company and if it was making profit over a longer period. This is called **speculation,** and it can be dangerous.

Speculation means _____.

Middle class: The growth of industry (1800s) changed the way people lived. The biggest social change was the growing importance of the middle class. The **middle class** was made up of businesspeople. Some of these people owned factories, mines, railroads, and banks.

Middle class means _____.

Anarchist: The State's Attorney said here that "Anarchy" was on trial. Anarchism and Socialism are as much alike, in my opinion, as one egg is to another. They differ only in their tactics. The **Anarchists** have abandoned the way of liberating humanity which Socialists would take to accomplish this. I say: Believe no more in the ballot, and use all other means at your command. (from speech by George Engel, condemned Haymarket Anarchist, 1886)

Engel describes *anarchism* as _____.

Foot binding. Women had always been subservient to men in Chinese society. One sign of their changing status (900s) was the new custom of **binding the feet** of upper-class girls. When a girl was quite young her feet were bound tightly with cloth, which eventually broke the arch of her foot and curled all but the big toe under. This produced the prized "lily-foot."

The phrase *foot binding* means _____.

FIGURE 5.2. Examples of vocabulary definitions from history textbooks.

used frequently so students develop the habit of checking the new terms and assessing their readiness for learning the concepts. This same Knowledge Rating can be used as a posttest, too. When given both before and after the study students have a graphic way to evaluate their learning.

Semantic Clustering

This simple pre-assessment helps students think about new concept terms by relating them to others. Rather than just identifying a single term, students are asked to connect each of the terms to one of the major categories that the teacher has identified on the graphic organizer (see the example in Figure 5.4). If students seem familiar with the topic of study or appreciate a challenge, this activity can be done by having them chunk the terms according to their own categories. Several teachers have turned this into a partner activity so students not only see the words visually, but also are encouraged to discuss them orally. When there are ELs in the group, this can be a very nonthreatening way for them to hear the same words repeated several times before they are introduced in the lessons.

The Mongol Conquests

Directions: All of the words listed below are important in our study of the Mongols. As you look through the list, check your level of familiarity with each of them and mark the box that best fits your understanding. If you feel you know a term well, then write a definition or provide an example of it in the box on the right. We will be using these words regularly, so take time to develop a way to study and practice those you don't know well now. At the end of the unit we will do this same activity and you should be able to identify how much you have learned.

Name _____ Period _____

Term	Know it well	Have seen but . . .	New to me	Definition
Pastoralist				
Clan				
Genghis Khan				
Mongolica				
Steppe				
Nomadic				
Mongol				
Khanate				
Persia				

FIGURE 5.3. Rate Your Knowledge Chart. The teacher identifies key terms that students will need to know and use as they learn the content of the unit or topic. These terms are then listed on a matrix for students to use as they prepare to study the content. Both the teacher and the students can use the responses to determine how much attention needs to be given to learning the terms/concepts. At the end of the unit or topic of study students can return to this same activity and evaluate how well they have learned the new concepts.

Directions: Choose words from the lists below and put them under the appropriate category or concept. Use as many of the words as you know and use each word only once. Some categories will have blank spaces even though you use all the words. If there are some terms you don't know at all, just circle them and you can add them to your "word-learning list" later.

The Great Depression

speculation	imported goods	deficit federal spending	mortgage payments	foreclosures	recovery	recession
tariffs	capital	business cycle	crash	Say's law	supply and demand	boom
unemploy-ment	over-production	economics	flawed economy	financial collapse	downward economic spiral	belief in business cycles

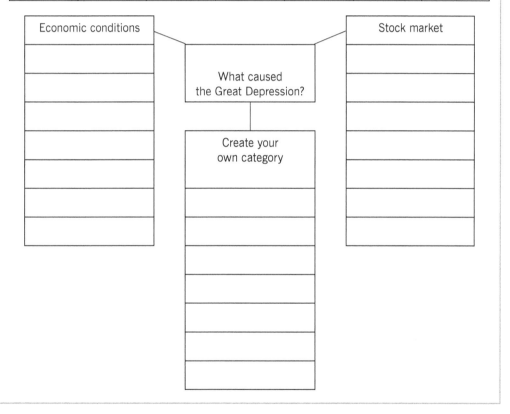

FIGURE 5.4. Concept Web. The teacher determines the key terms students will need to know and use during the unit or chapter/lessons. These words are listed for students, and their task is to sort the words using the categories provided on their worksheet. If the students are more knowledgeable about the topic, the teacher may ask them to create their own categories as they sort the terms. If that is the teacher's choice, then the boxes should be left free of labels.

Morphology Identification

As students enter secondary school they encounter more terms that derive from Greek and Latin roots and many others that have many syllables that carry meaningful morphemes (prefixes, roots, and suffixes). Students are more likely to include efforts to look at the component parts of words that are new to them when teachers focus on this resource for word learning. By giving short pre-assessments in which students are asked to divide key words for the unit/lesson into meaningful parts, they are reminded to use this strategy and to refresh their understanding of new terms by attending to the word parts (see Figure 5.5). Students come to secondary classrooms with a wide range of familiarity with how morphemes work in words. This assessment helps teachers learn more about students' familiarity with word parts and also permits teachers and students to set goals for expanding students' store of known morphemes.

The activity works best on unit terms that have familiar morphemes that are encountered in more than one word. For example, the suffixes -or and -er indicate that a person is being identified as in *surveyor, embalmer, teacher*, and so forth.

Alphabet Abundance

An enjoyable alternative to individual preassessments is the Alphabet Abundance activity that involves the whole class or a group of students working together. This is a variant on Allen's Predicting ABC's Chart (2000). This activity centers on students brainstorming all the words they can think of related to the topic of study that is being introduced. The teacher can be the scribe as students call out words they think are associated with the topic, writing the words on the chalkboard or on a SMART Board that all can view. The brainstorming is organized by having students contribute words in alphabetical order, starting with words that begin with *a*, then *b*, and on throughout the alphabet. An alternative to the whole-group activity is to divide the class into four or six groups, each of which is assigned one segment of the alphabet. For example, if six groups are identified, then each group has a section of four or more letters: one group does letters *a–d*; others do *e–h*; *i–l*; *m–p*; *q–t*; *u–z* (with the last group having more letters, but fewer likely words). See Figure 5.6 for an example of how these words can be recorded and assessed.

Exclusion Brainstorming

Another way to quickly activate students' thinking of the vocabulary they will need to use during a unit/extended lesson is for the teacher to create a list of words, most of which are important to the content, but to include in the list some that are not. The fun task for students, either working in pairs or small groups, is to identify each

Directions: As we learn new vocabulary terms it is often helpful to look at the parts of the unfamiliar words to see if there are any meaningful parts (prefix, root, suffix) that can help us determine the meaning. For example, what does it mean if you buy something that is imported? If you break this word into parts you can figure out what it means. Use the boxes to break each of the words into their meaningful parts. Then write what you think the word means.

im = into	*port* = carry	*ed* = happened in past

So the word *imported* probably means that something was carried into or brought into some place from somewhere else.

Use the boxes to break each of the words into their meaningful parts. Then write what you think the word means.

1. Dehydrate

Probably means _____

2. Decomposing

Probably means _____

3. Embalmer

Probably means _____

4. Pictogram

Probably means _____

Add in the same way:
     Archeologist
     Egyptologist
     Hieroglyphs

FIGURE 5.5. Morphology pre- and postassessment.

A–D	E–H	I–L
discrimination Constitution Amendment #16 battles churches blacks courts	freedom riders governors foes friends	leaders Little Rock Klu Klux Klan killings lynchings
M–P	**Q–U**	**V–Z**
marches protest Martin Luther King, Jr. Memphis Montgomery ministers police	songs (of movement) *To Kill a Mockingbird*	*Watsons Go to Birmingham* youth

FIGURE 5.6. Abundant Alphabet. This example comes from a class that was beginning their study of the 1960s Civil Rights movement. Six groups of students each worked for 10 minutes, which included time to talk about images they have of the time period before generating the words to construct their part of the alphabet. When students shared their lists with the whole class, it was clear there was a moderate amount of knowledge about some aspects of the Civil Rights movement. However, the teacher wanted students to think more deeply, so she asked the teams to return to their tables and scan through some of the newspaper articles she had planned to have them read next. Their task was to identify more terms and phrases that could be important.

word orally and decide whether it belongs in the discussion of the topic. If students think it does belong, they write the term in a sentence reflecting the possibility of what it means. If they decide it does not belong they cross it out. See the example in Figure 5.7.

Deepening Understanding of Key Domain-Specific Terms

Prereading activities help draw students' attention to the important vocabulary they will need to make sense of the content they study. However, it is also important that students are given opportunities to develop their understanding and use of these terms throughout the unit or lesson sequence. We have found three foci most helpful.

First, students benefit when they develop their own collections of words they are studying. They can do this in a vocabulary notebook or in a section of the social studies work (on computer or paper). It is important that the students not only write the words and, as is often the case, a short definition, but also create space for

---

Vocabulary and Phrases about the Great War

Directions: Decide which of the following words and phrases will be important as we study the Great War (World War I). For those that you think belong write a sentence using each on the back side of this paper. Those you think do not belong should be crossed out.

Militarism	Forging pacts
Popular culture	Allied forces
Crisis	Triple alliance
Machine gun	Ethnic conflict
Chlorine gas	Stalemate
Globalization	Stoicism
Rival alliances	Pacifism
Triple entente	Continental war
Mass media	Bismarck

FIGURE 5.7. Exclusion Brainstorming.

elaborating on the meaning by copying sentences where the term is used in varying ways, noting synonyms and antonyms for the word, and drawing, illustrating and connecting the word to other concepts/experiences. In creating entries for new terms many teachers find the Concept of Definition Map (Schwartz & Raphael, 1986) useful so students realize learning a definition is not learning just a synonym for the target word, but rather learning a word requires thinking of attributes, examples, and negative instances. (See Chapter 4, pp. 61–62 for an example.) The Vocabulary Four Square Model is another tool that achieves this same purpose. (See Chapter 6, p. 113 for an example.) Finally, Marzano's framework (2004) for word learning is also comprehensive; it suggests that after the teacher identifies a term and provides a description or example of the term, the students then restate or describe (not define) the term using their own words. Then they create a visual illustration (nonlinguistic representation) of the term and then keep track of the number of times they practice of the term.

Second, when students are actively involved in monitoring their expanding understanding of concepts they should also be given time to use these words orally in class. There are several easy ways to support students in this way. One is to use vocabulary practice for "bell ringer" activities. Students can be asked to Answer This!, a brief activity done with a partner. At the start of the class, the teacher writes a topical question on the board and each partner constructs a response using words and phrases from a list of terms on the word wall or in their vocabulary lists for the unit/lesson. Students share these with their partners and finally the teacher asks for some to also share their answer/s with the whole class.

A variation is to use the Think–Pair–Share (McTighe & Lyman, 1988) activity. The teacher poses a question, then each student thinks and writes his/her response and turns to a partner to share what they have written and to discuss their ideas together. Finally, the teacher asks some of the partners to share their ideas with the whole group. An even more basic format is for the teacher to write two or three words on the board and ask each student to "connect two" or "connect three" in a sentence that reflects what they are studying. Students can share their sentences first with partners or just with the whole group.

Involving students in more extended discussion of questions arising from their learning can also provide a focused way for them to use their developing academic vocabularies. While many teachers do conduct regular interactive discussions as part of their teaching, many teachers find they rely on a subset of the class in these exchanges. It can be more inclusive if these discussions are periodically based on some prepreparation by students. Students who are shy about speaking out in class as well as ELs derive much benefit from time to think about key questions before engaging in class discussions. The Discussion Web (Alvermann, 1991) is a powerful tool for just this. After students have developed some understanding about the topic of study that includes awareness of differing perspectives (through reading, viewing, or attending lectures) the teacher constructs a graphic with the question for discussion in the center. On either side are spaces for reasons for and against the premise. Students are given the web and must complete it before the class discussion. Many teachers make this a partner or shared project; students can search through the resources they have read or viewed to find support for both positions. Their task is not to argue only one side of the issue, but to provide reasons (evidence) supporting both sides of the issue. There is a section on the organizer for students to also record their conclusion or answer to the question.

Procon.org is a free, nonprofit resource designed to offer readers resources on controversial issues. Middle school teachers might want to check out Word Generation, which offers online units designed around "discussion dilemmas." These units are specifically designed to support academic vocabulary learning.

Figure 5.8 is an example of a Discussion Web that can be adapted for any topic. On the day of the discussion the teacher prechecks each student's web. The discussion then proceeds with the teacher calling on partners to share one reason or support for one side of the issue, and then to other groups to respond with evidence or reasons on the other side. By having carefully prepared their webs before class, all students can feel comfortable reporting on what they have written. As the discussion proceeds students can also be encouraged to check off reasons/evidence that others contribute to avoid unnecessary repetition of ideas. This web works well when teachers use document-based questions (DBQs) with primary source materials; they find this tool useful so students can record and evaluate evidence on the topic as they review documents.

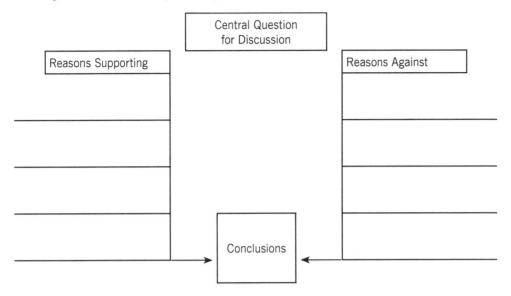

FIGURE 5.8. Discussion Web.

Finally, it is very helpful to encourage students to bring in examples of how the words they are learning are used in other contexts. Students can make copies of websites, cartoons, and media that use the words. Finding important terms while listening to radio news helps students recognize the value of their attention to vocabulary. When possible, teachers create a space for a collection of these word "citings" from these and other more traditional sources—newspaper, magazine, books, and advertisements as well as song lyrics and raps. Students can submit "citings" they come across to a class Twitter account; these words and phrases can be compiled on a class web page or blog. Encouraging students to look beyond the confines of their academic courses for the same vocabulary has a positive impact on their word learning and their sensitivity to language more generally.

The vocabulary-focused activities outlined above are useful and enjoyable ways to alert students to the important domain-specific terms they need to attend to as they are learning. However, it is also clear that there is no way history/social studies faculty can provide direct instruction on all the words that students need to learn. Much of the vocabulary learning that will occur comes informally, from listening, talking, and reading. That is why it is useful to include some time to read aloud to students from challenging documents and current affairs articles. It is also very helpful to include requirements or recommendations for students to also read a variety of types of texts on the same topic or theme (Ogle, 2010). The more they read the more likely it is that they will encounter the same concepts and terms that are important in new contexts. These experiences help students expand and refine their understanding of how the terms can be and are used.

Challenges in Teaching Vocabulary

Considering the number of domain-specific terms and phrases students need to learn as they consider issues in history and society it is also no wonder teachers can be frustrated in determining how to deal with this area. It is impossible to teach all of the terms students need to know individually.

It is also true that the idea of matching one word with a single definition will not be very useful in social studies. The meanings of concepts like *representative democracy, consensus,* and *constitutional government* keep expanding as students encounter them again and again—in learning about the American Revolution and the formation of the U.S. government, and throughout the study of American history and government.

How can teachers be most effective in helping students develop the academic vocabulary they need to read, write, and engage in academic discourse in social studies content across the grades? As Jeff Zwiers (2008) explains, "We could spend all day, every day on teaching new content words in research-based ways, but this would take the place of other necessary instruction. Or we could never teach words at all, and let them just sink in—we hope. As usual, we must find the right balance. We achieve this balance when we teach words as tools for understanding and for communicating meaning in our content areas" (p. 188). We agree with Zwiers that there needs to be a balance between building students' academic vocabularies and teaching the content. Teachers need to pay attention to the terms that are critical to the disciplinary content being learned, as well as attention to the precise uses of language that help students not only learn the content, but also develop general academic vocabulary and an interest in and awareness of the role of key terms. Recent research by Scott and her colleagues with middle-grade students (Scott, Flinspach, & Vevea, 2011; Scott, Miller, & Flinspach, 2012) underscores the fact that students need to know a large corpus of words to be successful in social studies learning. With the breadth of content that can be taught, and the frequent lack of agreement on the focus for instruction in the major areas of history, geography, economics, and government, teachers can feel adrift in determining what to teach and to what depth. Given this lack of agreement about many areas of the social studies curriculum, the vocabulary focus needs to evolve from and support the decisions that are made about the content to be taught and learned. When teachers engage in joint planning across several grade levels, more coherence and deeper student learning can be achieved.

Perspectives on Discipline-Based Vocabulary

Because word learning is an ongoing process of deepening and expanding important disciplinary concepts in social studies and history, there are several ways faculty can help students deepen their learning that can be effectively used in conjunction with a focus on learning individual terms. Words are learned more deeply when students build associations among terms and create a framework in their mind within which new concepts can be related to other knowledge and ideas. Combining contextual and definitional approaches has been shown to be most effective than either used alone (Baumann, Edwards, Boland & Font, 2012).

Developing Relationships among Terms

Words are learned best when they build on students' prior knowledge and can be related to other known words and concepts. For example, when students are studying forms of government, they can learn to analyze words like *monarchy*, *democracy*, and *autocracy* and separate the parts that indicate the type of government each is; they can also learn the meaning of *-racy* and analyze the change from *monarch* to *monarchy*.

As students become attentive to the key terms being introduced, they need to understand those in relation to the concepts being developed, and then to create some associations and links so they can retain those terms in meaning and in pronunciation. For example, as students learn about various land forms or social organizations (clans, tribes, nations, etc.) it is helpful not to teach each term separately, but to also help students compare and contrast the words and then to also evaluate what they learn against their personal experiences. If there are students from multiple countries in the class this type of comparative elaboration on the forms of government can be even more interesting.

Students can register to use the free version of Lucidchart (*www.lucidchart.com*) to generate and share concept maps. These concept maps can help them chart the relationships of key terms. Additional similar resources are listed in Chapter 7.

Another way to help students relate terms is to focus on the underlying structural and conceptual elements. For example, there is no reason for students to learn the concept *federal* as a single word. Rather, teachers can ask students to create a cluster of words that all share that same core word. They may locate *federalist*, *antifederalist*, *federalism*, and *new federalism*. A further interesting step is to explore the etymology of the term. Using the Web-based resource *www.etymologyonline.com* students would learn that federal is a word derived from Latin developed as a theological term for a covenant among religious people. The root is *fides*, or faith in Latin. They could then compare the shifting meanings of federal with the term *league* as used in the Iroquois League of Nations or the post-World War I League of Nations. Why weren't either of these called a *federation*? And the exploration can continue. Learning about words can lead in many directions and capture students' interests and memories in diverse ways. Figure 5.9 illustrates the affixes and combining forms that are frequently encountered in social studies texts. By working together across grade levels, teachers can help students learn to identify and use the meanings of these word parts in building their understanding of important terms and also help encourage their questioning of how words come into use, grow, and change their meanings and uses.

Linking Concepts across Time

Attention to concepts, like those of government or social organization, can also be deepened when students see how these concepts evolve and change over time. Students might use online comic strip generators (*www.makebeliefscomix.com/Comix*) to illustrate the progression of key concepts in a social studies or history class. They also may use these to illustrate core concepts. Creating a time line showing various important examples of developments and changes in a key concept can help many students better understand how concepts evolve and how, as a result, meanings for terms shift. A time line of the way maps identify the western part of what is now the United States can lead into an interesting study; students can read novels and poetry from various historical periods and elaborate their understanding of how this area of the country was labeled and why those labels changed. In our current context in the United States, it is worthwhile to explore how terms like *equality, franchise, inalienable rights, independence,* and *opportunity* have different connotations over time. Examining historical documents with a critical eye to whom or what the writers refer is important if students are to comprehend their meanings.

Prefixes	Roots	Suffixes
a- (not, without)	*part* (section, component)	*-able*
im- (not)	*port* (carry)	*-age*
ex- (out, from)	*agri* (field)	*-al*
de- (out, away)	*continent*	*-ant*
inter- (between)	*aqua* (water)	*-ence*
anti- (against)	*anthro* (human)	*-hood*
arch- (original, chief)	*arch* (primitive)	*-ism*
contra- (against)	*chron* (time)	*-ist*
dia- (through, across)	*crat, cracy* (rule)	*-ment*
ethno- (race, nation)	*dem* (people)	
mid- (middle)	*poli* (city)	
pre- (before)	*pop* (people)	
under- (below)	*scribe* (write)	
uni- (single, one)	*struct* (build)	

FIGURE 5.9. Affixes and combining forms found in social studies texts. *Note:* Some suffixes form nouns (*suffrage*), adjectives (*portable*), adverbs (*westward*), or verb forms (*populate*). From Blachowicz, Fisher, Ogle, and Watts Taffe (2013). Copyright 2013 by The Guilford Press. Reprinted by permission.

Connecting to Narratives and Visual Sources

The concepts, the settings, and the human interactions at the heart of history and social sciences can often be understood better through reading or hearing participants' narratives of the events and by viewing visual images of what they are studying (August & Gray, 2010; Ogle, 2000). With the accessibility of video clips showing other lands, other peoples, and times students can often develop a richer visual framework within which they can connect new vocabulary terms that describe and define what they see. When students then create their own sketches and label them they are more likely to retain and refine the meanings. For many, visual memories are stronger than verbal ones; for ELs this can be a particularly strong support in their learning. Teachers have used interactive whiteboards successfully to involve students in creating visual images of key terms. This can be done either individually or collaboratively, and the images can then be saved for future reference.

A Reminder about General Vocabulary

Every teacher needs to make decisions about what attention to give the development of key terms and how to do so most effectively. We have suggested throughout this book that it helps for teachers to think of academic words in two key categories (see Chapter 1): *general academic terms* and *domain-specific terms*. Doing so makes it possible to focus some attention on those general academic terms that can be used across content-area instruction. These are terms students need to complete their assignments and are also keys to their successful performance on high-stakes tests. For example, students can develop their facility with the academic terms *point of view, claims, analyze, illustrate, distinguish, justify,* and *contrast* not only in social studies, but also as they study science, math, and ELA. It is also important to check whether these general terms are used in specific and idiosyncratic ways in history/social studies, and then to explain these particular uses to students. When social studies texts and assessments ask students to "interpret the past," a specific approach is expected: Students need to use and reference evidence from texts, news articles, primary sources, and other data, not just to share their personal interpretations based on their own experiences. Some of the general academic terms include:

- *Analyze*: Describe the relationship of. . . .
- *Cite*: Mention or say the words of another as support for an idea.
- *Employ*: Apply knowledge of. . . .
- *Evaluate*: Judge something carefully using criteria.
- *Integrate*: Combine 2 or more ___ to create something new.
- *Explain*: Analyze interactions between. . . .
- *Contrast*: Use a spatial perspective to. . . .

- *Identify*: Understand historical chronology.
- *Chart*: Understand and create timelines showing events chunked in periods and eras.
- *Describe*: Understand and apply knowledge of historical thinking, chronology, and so on, to evaluate how history shapes the present and future.
- *Justify*: Use evidence to support a position or idea.

These more general academic terms can be developed over time and across disciplines, although teachers must take care to demonstrate variations on how the processes are enacted in each content area. The terms listed above refer to the kinds of thinking students are expected to use when exploring and learning new content; if students do not understand what is expected when asked to demonstrate what they know in these ways they may not succeed, but for the wrong reason—lack of understanding of the processes and formats.

It is also important that disciplinary teachers help students by highlighting some of the specific ways the more general thinking process terms are used in history/social studies, economics, and geography. The CCSS in history/social studies use many of these terms to define the specific ways students need to think about the content they are learning. Figure 5.10 lists several of the terms and phrases in the CCSS for history/social studies. As you read over these, think of the task confronting an EL who needs to understand the particular expectations embedded in these phrases. For example, will such students know what they are expected to do when asked to evaluate authors' differing points of view by assessing the authors' claims, reasoning, and evidence? These directions for how to engage with texts and authors need to be carefully explained and modeled for students.

Concluding Thoughts

So much of what our students need to know about the world around them and their own identity, as well as the challenges and opportunities they have to make a difference is grounded in history and the social sciences. It is critical that we design curriculum and learning experiences so students are motivated and fully engaged in meaningful learning activities; and so they can understand our history, geography, civics, economic, and political realities. And at the heart of each discipline's expectations is students' development of the concepts/vocabulary and discourse-specific ways of expressing ideas that will not only help them learn about the topics under study, but also will help them uncover new connections and relationships across time and space. Students deserve the best instruction we can provide. We hope this chapter can add in a small way to the instruction you provide in pursuit of this vision and goal.

Category of Anchor Standard	Sample of associated academic vocabulary and expectations
Reading standards	
Key Ideas and Details	*cite, textual evidence, analysis, primary and secondary sources, identify key steps in description of a process, evaluate, best accords*
Craft and Structure	*determine meaning of words and phrases. describe how text presents information, text, use structure (sequentially, comparatively, causally), analyze, identify point of view, loaded language, inclusion or avoidance of particular facts, point of view, differing points of view, author's claims, reasoning and evidence*
Integration of Knowledge and Ideas	*integrate, visual information, quantitative or textual analysis with qualitative, diverse formats and media, distinguish among . . . , evaluate premises, claims and evidence, corroborating or challenging, analyze relationship, integrate information into coherent understanding, note discrepancies*
Writing standards	
Text Types and Purposes	*arguments, discipline-specific content, support claims, logical reasoning, relevant, accurate data, credible sources, cohesion, clarify relationships among claims, counterclaims, reasons, and evidence, establish and maintain a formal style, objective tone, attend to norms and conventions of the discipline, provide concluding statement or section*
Production and Distribution of Writing	*coherent, styles appropriate to task, purpose and audience, address audience, shared writing*
Research to Build and Present Knowledge	*self-generated question, draw on several sources, generate additional related questions, multiple avenues of exploration, search terms, credibility and accuracy, quote or paraphrase, avoid plagiarism, standard format for citation, draw evidence, analysis, reflection, research*

FIGURE 5.10. Key CCSS Anchor Standard categories for history/social studies and associated academic vocabulary.

CHAPTER 6

Teaching Academic Vocabulary in Mathematics and Science

When students come to math and science classes they face the challenge of learning vocabulary that is different from most content areas. Math and science words tend to be long and look complex. There are many words with letter combinations that students do not see very often in other subjects, such as *vertex, rhombus, amphibious*. There are words that they will only see in math (*radian*) or in science (*organelle*), words they have seen or heard that will have new meanings (*improper*), and words that are combined in phrases to make new meanings (*lowest common multiple*). These words may often represent abstract concepts or complex processes, making instruction difficult. Teachers in these disciplines often tell us that the hardest thing to do is teach vocabulary, partly for these reasons. However, vocabulary instruction is helped by the fact that:

- Terms have very specific definitions (a *rhombus* is always a four-sided plane figure).
- Terms in a semantic domain may be defined in comparison to other terms in the same domain (a *vacuole* is always an *organelle*).

In relation to the *teaching* of the words:

- Concepts occur several times in any one lesson, and over several lessons, so that students repeatedly hear and use a word in different ways.
- Teaching vocabulary in math and science often involves demonstration, visual representation, and manipulation.

This chapter explores these and other characteristics of math and science vocabulary and suggests teaching strategies that will help students engage with these complex terms.

Implications of the CCSS in Math and Science

The CCSS include Reading Standards in Science and Technical Subjects K–12 that emphasize on the teaching and learning of vocabulary. For example, Standard 4 for grades 6–8 states that students will be able to "determine the meaning of symbols, key terms, and other domain-specific words and phrases as they are used in a specific scientific or technical context relevant to *grades 6–8 texts and topics*" (NGA & CCSSO, 2010a, p. 62). The CCSS for Mathematics do not explicitly address vocabulary, but such knowledge is implicit. For example, for Standard 6 students need to "attend to precision," and the standard includes the following: "Mathematically proficient students . . . use clear definitions in their discussion with others and in their own reasoning. They state the meaning of the symbols they choose" (NGA & CCSSO, 2010b, p. 7). In other words, students need to learn to use precise terminology to demonstrate their understanding of the subject matter—the accuracy of their language reflects the accuracy of their mathematical reasoning.

At the heart of word knowledge in math and science is that terms create boundaries around concepts, and allow us to name and understand them. Knowing words allows us to organize our knowledge in new ways, and to develop methods of manipulating those words to create a mathematical or scientific discourse.

Key Understandings about Math and Science Vocabulary

Teachers of math and science have always taught vocabulary—they have taught the major concepts in their discipline. Words are only one way in which these concepts can be presented, so it is important to think of vocabulary knowledge in these disciplines as being more than word knowledge, but rather knowledge of meanings. We want students to know the meaning of the word *trapezoid,* but we also want them to recognize when a plane figure is a trapezoid, how it differs from other plane figures, and how it can be used in mathematical reasoning. Complex concepts are part of the general complexity in math and science, so teaching meanings can take time and repetition. Another characteristic of vocabulary in math and science is that words are often learned as part of a semantic network—a unit of study on *tropism* may include the term, *phototropism, thermotropism, geotropism,* and more. Such words can be easily linked and may even be defined in relation to each other. A third characteristic is that many words that students come across have more than one meaning. The word *improper* in the term *improper fractions* has no clear connection to *improper behavior.* Each of these characteristics will be addressed in more depth.

Complexity

All content areas contain complex concepts that may be unfamiliar to students; these concepts can be abstract (*solar energy*) or expressed in phrases (*associative property of addition; line plot*). As teachers of a discipline, it is our job to teach students about the important concepts in our subject area. We need to be as efficient as possible in making the complex simple. We know that abstract terms are more difficult to teach than concrete terms (*photosynthesis* as compared to *stamen*), so we may need to spend more time teaching them. Science includes a great deal of classification, and while teaching the members of a class might be easy, teaching the nature of a class can be more difficult. Finally, while students may think they know the meaning of individual words in a phrase, the combination of those words may be describing a complex concept: *line plot.*

The density of complex words in a text affects comprehension (Nagy, Anderson, & Herman, 1987). For example:

> The coefficients of a chemical equation indicate the relative number of particles and the relevant number of moles of reactants and products. (Wilbraham et al., 2005, p. 364)

This example demonstrates that our knowledge of the subject matter determines which terms we consider to be complex. To a non-chemist the terms *coefficients, relative, particles, verbal, moles, reactants,* and *products* (seven of the 22 words) may all seem complex; this reflects a high degree of concept density. To a chemist, or a student who has been well prepared for this unit, perhaps only one of two of those words would seem complex in the context of instruction. As teachers we are sometimes so familiar with our subject that we can forget how many terms may be unfamiliar to our students. For example, in the sentence *Because of the wide range of organisms, scientists classify organisms so that the study of them can be simplified* (Watkins & Leto, 1994), we might focus our instruction on the important terms *organisms* and *classify.* While these are important, we need to recognize that for many students the terms *wide range, study of,* and *simplified* may also lead to difficulty in understanding the text.

Science texts often contain multimorphemic words (*micro + organ + ism*) in conceptually dense sentences. Such words may pose issues of decoding that need to be addressed even prior to deconstructing the meaning of the sentence. However, such words provide an opportunity to teach and reinforce knowledge of important morphemes.

Mathematics texts may contain phrases with complex grammatical patterning that result in complex meaning relationships.

> An altitude of a prism is a segment that has endpoints in the planes containing the bases and that is perpendicular to both planes. The height of a prism is the length of an altitude. (Schultz, Hollowell, Ellis, & Kennedy, 2004, p. 407)

The first sentence is typical of definitional sentences in math. It contains extended noun phrases (*planes containing the bases*) that are qualifiers of other nouns (*segment*). However, even complex terms in math and science have *precise* meanings. If students understand each of the terms in the above definition (*segment, endpoint, planes, bases, perpendicular*) then the meaning of *an altitude of a prism* is not ambiguous (and a diagram disambiguates it even further). In a simpler example, the *associative property of addition* has only one meaning, although its application can seem complex. In other words, once the meaning of a term has been introduced, the basic meaning remains the same, even when the nature of the concept itself is expanded. For example, a *triangle* is always a three-sided plane figure, even when we add knowledge of particular types of triangles and the properties of triangles. This makes it easier to develop understanding of already familiar concepts as students advance through the grades.

General and Domain-Specific Vocabulary: A Specific Example of Complexity

The CCSS makes the distinction between domain-specific vocabulary, that is, the concepts in a content area (*theme, point on a graph*), and general academic vocabulary, or words that can be applied across content areas (*consist of, describe*). Is this is false dichotomy? Some have questioned whether the meaning of supposedly general academic terms is the same across subject areas. In an analysis of the Academic Word List (Coxhead, 2000), Hyland and Tse (2007) found that there was little overlap in meanings across the subject areas for words supposedly common to more than one discipline. The general meaning of a term may describe different processes in different subjects. For example, although the word *analyze*—defined as "to resolve or separate a whole into its elements or component parts"—shares a common meaning across subject areas, the actual application differs. If we look for examples of the use of the word *analyze* in different standards we can see that the application takes very different forms.

ELA Standards

- Determine central ideas or themes of a text and *analyze* their development . . .
- *Analyze* how and why individuals, events, and ideas develop and interact in the course of a text.
- *Analyze* how specific words choices shape meaning or tone.

Math Standards

- Make sense of problems and persevere in solving them. (*Analyze* givens, constraints, relationships, and goals.)
- Construct viable arguments and critique the reasoning of others. (*Analyze* situations by breaking them into cases, and recognizing and using counterexamples.)

What does this mean for instruction? Simply put, teachers will need to teach the meaning of the word *analyze* in the context of how it is being applied. The process of analyzing problems is not the same as analyzing character development. So teaching a meaning of *analyze* may be important in relation to differentiating it from *synthesize*, but teachers will still need to teach a specific meaning in relation to the content to which the process is being applied. This is true not only for *analyze*, but for many other words classified as "general academic vocabulary."

The Special Case of Learning Symbols

Students do not just have to learn the meaning of a concept in math and science; they may have to learn two representations of it (e.g., *greater than* and >). Mathematicians will tell you that mathematics has its own universal language, and that this language is expressed through symbols. Similarly, many science concepts, such as abbreviations (e.g., *Na* for *sodium*) and numbers on the periodic table of elements, are universal. Learning a symbol is similar to learning a new term for a familiar concept, except that in this case the concept and the symbol may be taught together. If students are already familiar with a concept, then teaching a new term does not require the number of repetitions and examples that are needed if both the concept *and* the term are new. Similarly, teaching a symbol may not require as much practice once the term becomes familiar. In fact, for many symbols (such as =), the icon may become more familiar than the spelled word for that concept.

Semantic Relatedness

As Hiebert and Cervetti (2012) put it, "The meaning of one conceptually complex word typically relies on an accurate (and precise) meaning of another complex word" (p. 338).

- Terms are often introduced as part of a unit of study (e.g., *heat capacity, specific heat*). How they are related is made apparent.
- Terms are often defined in relation to each other (e.g., *endothermic process* and *exothermic process*).

So, for example, in a high school chemistry unit on chemical reactions the terms *chemical equation, balanced equation,* and *skeleton equation* will be defined in relation to each other, and numerous examples given. In a geometry class, the terms *tangents, secants,* and *chords* will also be taught in relation to each other, and numerous diagrams used to make the meanings apparent.

Multiple Meanings

A contrast is often made in vocabulary instruction between teaching a new term for a familiar concept, teaching a new term for a new concept, and teaching a new meaning for a familiar term. The first may be the easiest, and the third the hardest. A brief examination of the terms in Figure 6.1 indicates some math terms that have a common meaning as well as a domain-specific meaning. Similarly, Figure 6.2 shows that science terms can also have a common meaning.

    Teachers may need to review the common meanings of some of these words prior to using them in math or science. A particular concern involves words that have a different meaning in two content areas. For example, in math one *balances an equation*, whereas in science *balance* is achieved when two *opposing forces* cancel each other out. Also, in this instance, students probably come to school thinking of *balance* as something they do on a wall (or similar). The issue with words such as this, which *might* be considered part of a general academic vocabulary, is that it may only make sense to teach the meaning specific to the content area in relation to other concepts in the unit of study. Why would we attempt to teach the mathematical term *balance* in a context other than when we are teaching equations?

Grade 6		Grade 7		Grade 8	
ratio	*order of*	*proportion*	*surface area*	*terminating*	*reflection*
tape diagram	*operations*	*simple interest*	*sample*	*decimal*	*translation*
greatest	*substitution*	*tax*	*population*	*repeating*	*similar figures*
common	*nets*	*markup*	*probability*	*decimal*	*corresponding*
factor	*median*	*markdown*	*frequency*	*irrational*	*angles*
property	*mode*	*gratuities*	*tree diagram*	*number*	*interior*
integer	*range*	*commissions*		*square root*	*exterior*
positive	*mean*	*scale drawing*		*cube root*	*scatter plot*
number	*opposite*	*plane sections*		*radical*	*input*
negative	*absolute value*			*slope*	*rotation*
number	*term*				

High school number and quantity		High school algebra	High school functions
imaginary number		*maximum*	*domain*
real number		*minimum*	*range*
polar form		*remainder theorem*	*relative maximum*
quadratic equation			*end behavior*
initial point			*periodicity*
terminal point			*rate of change*
zero matrix			*step function*
			period

FIGURE 6.1. Math terms with common meanings.

Grade 6		Grade 7		Grade 8	
bias	acid rain	bond	age	calorie	boundary
boiling point	atmosphere	charge	cast	conservation	class
cell	belt	code	continental	fiber optics	family
efficiency	community	concentration	shelf	frequency	host
element	consumer	conductor	contour	gamma rays	order
energy	crest	control group	nervous system	interference	primary
independent	crust	direct current	reflection	light year	product
law	jet stream	field	relative	luster	reaction
mass	key	lever	resistance	matter	regular
model	kingdom	machine	solar wind	pitch	specific heat
natural	niche	mixture	tissue	power	
net force	plane	neutral	water table		
simple	rain shadow	period	work		
substance	revolution	product			
trough	revolve				
wave	speed				
wedge	water cycle				

High school
physical property, canopy, climax community, understory, buffer, indicator, base, catalyst, law of constant composition, chemical reaction, coefficient, subscript, ideal gas, lattice, polar, group, expected yield, significant digit, mole, principal investigation, elasticity, mechanical energy, half-life, core, joint, brain stem, body cavity, organ, concentration gradient, active site, resting potential, behavior, carrying capacity, food web, food chain, analogous structures, competition, solution, transport, aerobic, fermentation, analogous

FIGURE 6.2. Science terms with common meanings.

Communication, Discussion, and Writing

The Next Generation Science Standards (National Research Council, 2011) move away from using the term *inquiry-based science* to identifying a set of science- and engineering-based practices, although it can be argued that these practices refine and deepen the meaning of the term *inquiry* (Lee, Quinn, & Valdes, 2013). Embedded within these practices is the ability to communicate ideas. Similarly, the CCSS for Mathematics (NGA & CCSSO, 2010b) incorporate communication as an important component. There is a wealth of research to support the idea of discussion as a means of developing communication in both math and science (Countryman, 1992; Sampson, Enderle, Grooms, & Witte, 2013). We believe that students need talk about and use the vocabulary of math and science in order to learn it and refine their understanding. In subsequent sections we present some ways in which students can do this effectively. In addition, students need to communicate mathematical and scientific ideas in writing (Grant & Fisher, 2010; Murray, 2004).

A national survey found that math teachers were less likely to do so than other teachers (Gillespie, Graham, Kiuhara, & Hebert, 2014), although all disciplinary teachers tended to use writing for mundane tasks, and not very often. We will make suggestions for incorporating writing in both math and science.

Key Understandings about Vocabulary Instruction in Math and Science

Given that the nature of the vocabulary to be learned is often more specific in math and science than in ELA, there are some characteristics of instruction that differ from those in ELA classrooms. In the latter, teachers are often concerned about which words to teach, and various ways of choosing appropriate words have been proposed. In math and science, the domain-specific vocabulary to be taught is usually specified in the curriculum. There is less variation in what is taught across classrooms, and specific meanings are often provided in textbooks and curriculum guides. To the extent that word choice is less of an issue, a teacher's task in relation to selecting words for word learning is that much easier. However, there is a caveat: The small words are often the ones that can cause difficulties. For example, *compare, design, look, work, average, equivalent, vary,* and *reasonable* are all words with common meanings that may have explicit meanings in math.

The Importance of Visual Representation

Math and science include more visual representations in textbooks than do language arts and social studies, and the frequency and variety of graphics has increased (Slough, McTigue, Kim, & Jennings, 2010). Such visuals are an integral part of instruction—not just in textbooks. However, even within a discipline the visual layouts in texts are not the same for each subject—for example, biology and physics display differences, as do algebra and geometry. So a brief comparison of a ninth-grade biology text with a high school geometry text would show that the former has diagrams or pictures that not only expand on content in the print, but also introduce new information. The latter, as might be expected, has few pictures, but every page is full of geometric figures that demonstrate concepts and processes. Both science and math texts include tables and charts in most units. The implications for instruction are that we need to teach students to interpret visual information, both in relation to information conveyed in the print and in terms of information that is only present in graphic form. As Moore-Russo and Shanahan (2014) explain, "Visual representations such as charts, graphs, diagrams, and figures distill and display complex relational information that is not always described in written text" (p. 529).

McTigue and Croix (2010) recommend having students practice the use of both print and visual forms by having them identify and chart information that is in the text only, in graphic form only, and in both. They suggest that, initially, few students are able to identify all the information and that continued modeling and discussion is needed to develop the ability to access both forms of information in a text. Moore-Russo and Shanahan (2014) draw a distinction between four types of representation of mathematical relationships: linguistic, algebraic, numeric, and graphic. They point out that students need to learn the nature of the information that is typically found in each form. So charts may be easiest form to extract specific data points, while graphic representations display patterns. The importance of this for vocabulary instruction is that students learn the meaning of concepts through more than linguistic representation—so "word" learning is only one form of understanding.

While visuals can be used for instruction, students may produce charts and other visual representation to demonstrate their learning. John is a high school biology teacher, and his classroom has charts and diagrams on all the walls. Some of them are produced professionally, and some are designed by his students. An example from the unit on cell structure and function is shown in Figure 6.3. John also has his students produce models of a cell, with the component parts labeled, for homework. Many of them use play dough; see, for example the model shown in Figure 6.4.

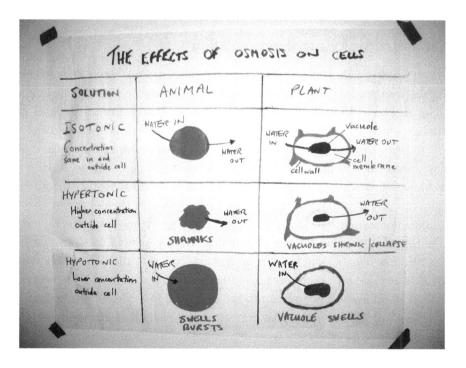

FIGURE 6.3. Classroom chart for osmosis.

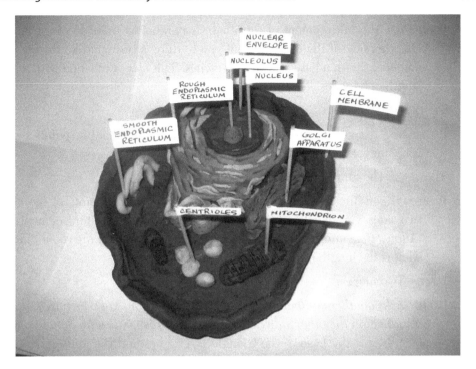

FIGURE 6.4. Model of an animal cell.

The Importance of Repetition and Review

We know that a word must be experienced repeatedly in different contexts to be learned (see Chapter 3). The word should be repeated both in one particular lesson and across lessons. Even though the following example comes from only one class period, you can see how the teacher and the students repeatedly use important terms in the course of the lesson. In the following high school geometry lesson, Julie is introducing *midsegments of triangles and trapezoids*.

Julie draws a triangle on the whiteboard and draws a segment whose endpoints are the midpoints of two sides.

JULIE: Today we are looking at midsegments. I am drawing a line from the midpoint of this side of the triangle to the midpoint of this side. What do you think it is called?

STUDENT: A midsegment.

JULIE: Good, what do you notice about the midsegment in relation to the other side of the triangle?

STUDENT: It is parallel.

JULIE: Yes, the midsegment of a triangle is parallel to the side of a triangle. OK, this side of the room, I want you to draw a triangle like this in your notebooks with a base length of 4 inches. This side, draw one with a base length of 6 inches.

STUDENTS: (*Draw.*)

JULIE: Now draw the midsegment parallel to the base. What two points should you connect?

STUDENT: The midpoints of the other two sides.

JULIE: OK—a line parallel to the base that joins the midpoints of the other two sides. Go ahead and do that, and then measure the midsegment. . . . (*Allows time and then asks a student on the first side of the room.*) James, what is the length of the midsegment you drew?

JAMES: Two inches.

JULIE: (*Asks another student, who also gives the response of 2 inches, and asks a student on the other side of the room, who responds with 3 inches.*) OK, on this side the base of the triangle is 4 inches and the midsegment is 2 inches long. On this side of the room the base is 6 inches, and the midsegment is 3 inches long. What can we hypothesize?

STUDENT: The midsegment is half the length of the base.

JULIE: Good—we can say that another way as a definition. (*Writes on whiteboard.*) A midsegment of a triangle is parallel to a side of the triangle and has a measure equal to one-half of that side. Any questions? OK, I want you to look in your text on page _____ and do activity 2 on the midsegment of a trapezoid [Figure 6.5].

Once the activity is complete, Julie asks students to compare their work to that of two other students. Then she leads a class lesson to generate a formula for finding the length of midsegment of a trapezoid, noting that when the short base

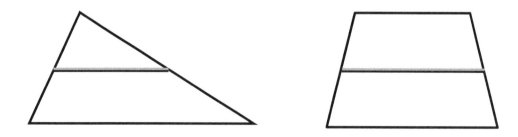

FIGURE 6.5. Midsegments of a triangle and of a trapezoid.

of a trapezoid is zero, then the formula can be used to find the midsegment of a triangle.

This lesson demonstrates how:

- A concept (*midsegment*) is introduced and reviewed over an extended period.
- The teacher and students continually review terms during a lesson.
- The teacher reinforces the concept through visual representation.

The Importance of Manipulation

Julie's lesson shows one way in which drawing and measuring instruments can be used as a form of manipulation to learn a new concept. In the next example lesson (adapted from a seventh-grade lesson by Wendy Mohrenweiser and Liz Gates), students were asked to decide which of two cylinders had the greater volume. They reviewed some important terms, such as *diameter, circumference, radius, pi*, and *area of a circle*, and discussed the relations among them. They then worked in groups, using rulers, tape, and calculators, to complete the problem sheet shown in Figure 6.6. Every person in the group had to write the same information and agree with it. In the left column, each step in the problem solution was written in words; in the right column, the math calculations were written in symbols. The students then shared their solutions with the class, using a projector. During this lesson, the important concepts were experienced repeatedly: they were heard, read, spoken, seen, written, manipulated, related to each other, and represented by symbols. In addition,

- The terms were applied in meaningful ways to solve a problem.
- Knowledge of the terms was built on previous understandings.
- Knowledge of the terms was extended.
- New knowledge was related to previous learning.

The linking of manipulation with use of the language is important in such learning experiences.

Visual representation, repetition, and manipulation are important in teaching and learning in math and science. Textbooks now are commonly linked to other resources, such as virtual labs, that support this learning. For example, in relation to the unit on cell structure, students could go online and manipulate parts of a cell, "view" a cell under a microscope with the parts identified, and view a video presentation on the topic. In addition to these components of a lesson, we now look at specific strategies for teaching word meaning. We have grouped these as: definitional and related maps, other clustering techniques, graphic organizers, and word structure.

Directions: Using two sheets of 8½″ × 11″ paper, construct two cylinders by sticking opposite edges together—one cylinder with a height of 11″ and one with a height of 8½.″ Which cylinder will have the greater volume, or will the volume be the same?

Prediction: _____

Use the table below to describe the steps your group used to solve the problem.

Step	Words	Math symbols
1		
2		
3		
4		
5		
6		
7		

Use the back of the paper for more steps. Be ready to share your solution with the rest of the class.

FIGURE 6.6. Volume of a cylinder problem.

Definitional and Related Maps

Mapping the meanings of words has been covered in other chapters. However, certain kinds of maps lend themselves to science and math.

Concept of Definition

In teaching a concept of definition, it is most appropriate to use a graphic, similar to a semantic web (Schwartz & Raphael, 1985). Figure 6.7 shows a concept of definition map (sometimes called a word web). The map follows the form of a traditional definition in that it contains the category to which the word belongs, the defining characteristics, and some examples. For this reason it is perfectly suited to math and science vocabulary.

The example in Figure 6.7 demonstrates the various components of a good definition. A quadrilateral belongs to the category of polygons. Its differentiating feature is that it has four sides. Notice how this feature distinguishes it from other polygons, like a triangle. When working with students, demonstrate that all items that might describe a term may not show how it differs from other words in that category. For example, a quadrilateral is a plane figure, but all polygons are plane figures, so that is not a distinguishing characteristic. You may notice in the figure that you could construct a separate definition map for each of the examples, or add to the map by including other polygons—triangle, hexagon, and so forth. Putting definition maps together can become an overview of the vocabulary in the whole unit of study. (See Chapter 7 for the links to some online mapping tools.)

Structured Overviews

Structured overviews work best when you are presenting concepts that are directly related through subordination and superordination. They work well in relation to the concepts presented in a text, but should not be limited to this. The basic pattern is presented in Figure 6.8, but variations can occur. The two advantages of structured overviews are that they present a graphical representation of the whole domain under study and they show hierarchical relationships among the concepts.

As with other maps, structured overviews may be presented only partly completed (as in the science example for energy in Figure 6.9). Students are required to fill in the missing terms after reading or learning in other ways. The advantage

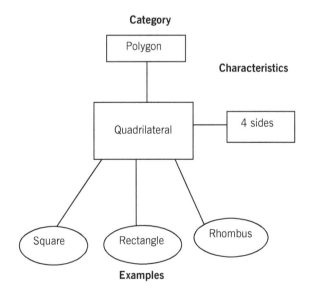

FIGURE 6.7. Concept of definition map (word web).

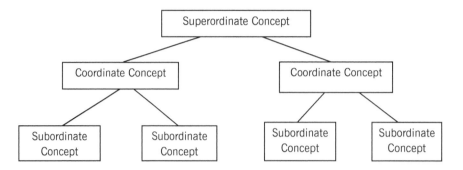

FIGURE 6.8. Components of a structured overview.

of a structured overview is it presents information in a way that formalizes the hierarchical relationships between concepts. The graphic form allows students to examine these relationships in a way no other format can.

Concept Circles

The basic idea here is to explore the relationships that exist between four important concepts in a subject area. The teacher divides a circle into four quadrants and places a concept in each quadrant (e.g., Figure 6.10). Students work individually or in pairs to describe or identify the relationship that exists. They engage in discussion to share their thinking. Sometimes, if this is a review activity, it is appropriate to leave a quadrant blank and ask the students to provide the missing term. Gay (2008) suggests other modifications for concept circles.

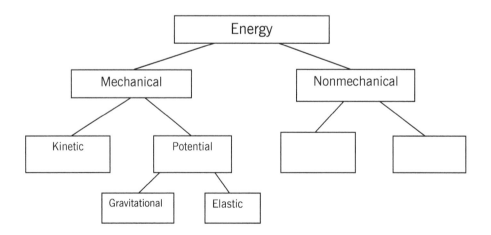

FIGURE 6.9. Structured overview for energy.

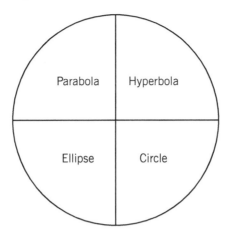

FIGURE 6.10. A concept circle.

A "Four-Square"

Some teachers like to use a simple rectangle divided into four sections as a way to ask students to move beyond just memorizing a definition. They ask students to write the word in one of the boxes, and then put information that will help them remember the meaning in the others. The example in Figure 6.11 shows a four-square for the term *vector*. In this diagram there is the definition, an example, and an image to help the student remember the meaning. A four-square may take various forms with the teacher deciding the categories of information. Alternatively, students can decide on what they want to include, perhaps using a template like that shown in Figure 6.12. You may think of some other variations that would be effective for your students and with your subject matter.

The Word	Definition
Vector	Physical quality that has both direction and magnitude.
Example	**Image**
30 m.p.h. northwest	

FIGURE 6.11. Vocabulary four-square for *vector*.

Directions: Write the word in the first space below. Choose three or more of the options in the boxes below to help you explore the word and get to know the word better.

The word	Textbook definition
Example	Non-example
Synonym	Antonym
Image	Related words
Morphemes	Etymology
Characteristics	Definition from dictionary

FIGURE 6.12. Template for various components of a four-square.

Other Clustering Techniques

Interactive Word Walls

Pat Cunningham, who has been credited with inventing word walls, says that it is not enough to have a word wall, you have to *do* a word wall (Cunningham, 2012). While this refers to word walls for primary grades, many teachers in all grades have taken her idea and work with students to implement and review word walls in all the content areas. *Doing* a word wall means reviewing the words on a regular basis so that students are reminded of the orthography and/or the meanings of the words posted. The nature of the posting itself may vary, but review is important. In John's high school biology classroom the students post the main concepts for each unit as they study it. Students take turns to write a concept on one side of a folded index card and the definition on the other. The card is posted on the word wall so that the word can be seen, but the fold has to be lifted to see the definition. John ensures that the concepts are arranged in meaningful categories, and for 2 or 3 minutes in each lesson selects words and asks students for their meanings. He always has two word walls at any one time—the current unit and the previous unit. The latter is not reviewed every day, but he returns to it at least once a week.

Some teachers use more visual information on their word walls. Jackson, Tripp, and Cox (2011) describe middle school classrooms where the students participate in the construction of word walls by providing visual information in the form of photographs and pictures to illustrate each concept. They argue that five characteristics are important:

1. Words are aligned with current instruction.
2. Words are visible from a distance.
3. Words are arranged to illustrate relationships and organize learning.
4. The wall contains student-generated material.
5. The visual supports are color photographs, pictures, or actual items (realia). (p. 47)

Word Sorts

This is sometimes called List–Group–Label, and this name summarizes its procedure, which asks students to examine a list words on a particular topic, group them, and then specify the criterion they have used for grouping with a label. For example, you could present students with terms from a unit on acceleration. The list might include these terms:

Motion
Frame of reference
Acceleration
Time interval
One-dimensional motion
Displacement
Free fall
Constant acceleration
Magnitude
Average velocity

Air resistance
Velocity
Direction
Instantaneous velocity
Terminal velocity

You could add to the difficulty of the task by including one or two terms from a previous unit, and allowing a "miscellaneous" category. Although there is no definitive number of words to use, keeping the list to about 25 words makes it manageable. If you provide the labels to the various categories (a closed sort) it provides direction to the students. Not providing the labels is sometimes termed an open sort. DeLuca (2010) suggests having students complete a closed sort by first providing them with the definitions of the main categories (e.g., *circulatory system, respiratory system, urinary system*). When given the rest of the terms to sort in groups, they can discuss how each term fits with a particular definition. Both open and closed sorting provide review of a topic, although they can also be used as a pre-unit activity. These word sorts can be completed collaboratively on an interactive board.

These two categorization exercises allow students to practice and develop their vocabularies without having to be concerned with definitions or supplying meanings. The categorizing itself supplies sufficient structure for students to begin to learn unfamiliar meanings or to refine their understanding of partially known meanings.

Exclusion Brainstorming

While this activity does not ask students specifically to cluster words in categories, it has similarities in terms of asking them to identify terms that do not belong to a specific class. For example, before a unit on work and energy, teachers might ask students to identify which words from the following list they would not expect to see in the unit.

Kinetic
Potential
Osmosis
Mechanical
Transfer
Vector
Magnitude
Displacement

Force
Chemical
Convex
Elastic
Conservation
Acceleration

Students might work in pairs to decide (in 3 minutes) which would be seen and which would not. The teacher could then go around the class asking each pair in turn about one word, and ask them to justify their response. This brief exercise helps the teacher determine how much students know about a topic, and also introduces the words to the students. The exercise can also be used to review terms learned in previous units (e.g., *vector, acceleration*).

Other Graphic Organizers

Semantic Feature Analysis

A semantic feature analysis is another graphic organizer that helps students remember the distinguishing characteristics of related terms. After working on a unit, the teacher may give students the terms and features and asked them to complete the chart, or may give them terms and ask them to put in the features themselves (Figure 6.13). The goal is for the completed chart to have no row the same. Students can then be asked, for example, as to what distinguishes a *square* from a *rhombus*. Since science and math are very precise in the meanings of terms, this type of chart works well to highlight what makes one member of a class different from another.

Quadrilaterals	Four sides	All sides equal	Opposite sides parallel	Opposite sides equal	Angles equal	Only one pair of parallel sides
parallelogram	X		X	X		
rectangle	X		X	X	X	
square	X	X	X	X	X	
rhombus	X	X	X	X		
trapezoid	X					X

FIGURE 6.13. Semantic feature analysis for quadrilaterals.

Box and T-Chart

Students have probably been asked from first grade onward to complete Venn diagrams to show the similarities and differences between two members of a class (e.g., *insects* and *spiders*). An alternative form of the same activity is a box and T-chart as shown in Figure 6.14. While both organizers ask students to compare and contrast terms, the latter is perhaps easier to complete, as students do not end up trying to squash words into small spaces.

Similarities	
Differences 1	**Differences 2**

FIGURE 6.14. Box and T-chart.

Word Structure

Teaching Morphemes

As a result of their work, Scott and her colleagues (2011) argue that academic vocabulary instruction in math and science benefits from a generative approach that includes the teaching of morphemes. A *morpheme* is the smallest unit of meaning in a language. For example, *cats* has two morphemes: *cat* and the plural *-s*. There are several common morphemes in math and science, some of which can be seen in Figures 6.15 and 6.16. Many math and science words consist of two or more morphemes—for example, *quadrilateral, crustaceans.*

Morpheme	Meaning	Math usage
ampl	large, wide	*amplitude, amplification*
centri, cenetri	center	*concentric, centripetal*
con	with, together	*converge, convert, conjoin*
equi	equal	*equidistant, equilibrium*
form	shape	*formula, uniform*
fract, frag	break	*fraction, fragment*
graph	written	*graph, graphic*
magn, maj	great	*magnitude, major, magnify*
medi	half, middle, between	*media, medium*
meter	measure	*meter, thermometer*
multi	many	*multiply, multiple*
numer	number	*numeral, numerator*
poly	many	*polyhedron, polygon*
rad	ray	*radius, radial*
sphere	ball, sphere	*Hemisphere*
Number	**Meaning**	**Math usage**
bi	two	*bilateral*
tri	three	*triangle, trisect*
quad	four	*quadrangle, quadrant*
hex	six	*hexagon, hexachord*
deca	ten	*decimal, decathlon*
kilo	thousand	*kilometer*

FIGURE 6.15. Common math morphemes.

Morpheme	Meaning	Science usage
astro	star	*astronomy, astronaut*
bio	life	*biology, biome, biosphere*
chlor	green	*chlorophyll, chloroplast*
eco	habitat	*ecology, ecosystem*
hydro	water	*hydrogen, hydroelectric*
meta	change	*metamorphosis, metabolism*
micro	small	*microscope, microorganism*
logy	science	*biology, geology, physiology*
photo	light	*photosynthesis, phosphorescent*
sym	together	*symmetry, symbiosis*
therm	heat	*thermal, thermometer*
vor	eat	*omnivore, carnivore, herbivore*

FIGURE 6.16. Common science morphemes.

Two basic processes may be appropriate for helping students develop morphological awareness: *decomposition* of words into their morphemes, and the *derivation* of complex words. In the first process, the students look at a word and decompose it to find the root word that would be appropriate in a phrase or sentence. The phrase or sentence scaffolds the task by providing meaning. For example, students could be asked to decompose the word *microscopic* in the heading "The Microscopic World of Viruses" in a science text. An additional part of the exercise could be to ask the students to indicate the morphemes by marking them in some way (drawing a box around them or using a highlighter). Decomposition is best taught by using several members of a word family—or instance, *photograph, photosynthesis, telephoto,* and *photogenic.* The second basic process is derivation, or putting morphemes together. This is harder and is best practiced with words students already know. They might be supplied with a list of morphemes that are prefixes and a list of roots; they might then be asked to combine them into words with which they are familiar, and to use those words in a sentence. When morphemes are taught, it is important for students to engage in the repetition and practice that are essential for all word learning. A special case for morpheme instruction can be made for cognates when teaching students whose first language is Spanish. If there is a common English word for the academic word, DeLuca (2010) suggests providing a three-column chart with the common English term in the first column, the academic English terms in the second column, and the Spanish terms in the third column (e.g., *body, corpus/corpse, cuerpo*). A list of some common Spanish cognates in math and science is shown in Figure 6.17, with a URL where a more complete list can be found.

antioxidant—antioxidante	curve—curva
atmosphere—atmósfera	absolute—absoluto
balance—balancear	simplify—simplificar
magnitude—magnitud	simultaneous—simultáneas
modify—modificar	equations—ecuaciones
sediment—sedimento	symmetrical—simétrica

FIGURE 6.17. Some science and math cognates (English and Spanish). Additional cognates by subject can be found at *http://spanishcognates.org*.

Writing

Writing is core to understanding in both math and science. It is through writing, which involves reflection and translation, that we come to understand fully what we have learned. In math, students have tended to learn to do problems by mimicking the example problems in the text, or those completed on the board by the teacher. Students can succeed "without ever understanding the concepts underlying the numerical acrobatics they have just learned to achieve" (Fletcher & Santoli, 2003, p. 3). Similarly in science, students can learn definitions and complete calculations without ever truly understanding the concepts and relationships in the unit of study. We are not saying that all students are this way, but many may be, despite efforts to reform the math and science curricula. Writing is time consuming, and teachers need to allow time for students to develop their thought beyond mimicking the teacher or the textbook. However, as in all forms of writing, students need models of what constitutes successful writing, so we need to be clear in our expectations and in providing good models for the process and the product.

Most students in science and math keep notebooks, and as teachers we have our own ideas as to what constitutes appropriate entries.

Science Notebooks

Teachers need to consider what elements of a science notebook are most appropriate to meet their learning goals in science. The website *www.sciencenotebooks. org* contains suggestions for organizing a notebook and samples of student work. The authors—the North Cascades and Olympic Science Partnership— recommend eight different types of entries:

1. Drawings
2. Tables, Charts, and Graphs
3. Graphic Organizers

4. Notes and Practice Problems
5. Reflective and Analytical Entries
6. Inserts
7. Investigation Formats
8. Writing Frames

Some of these have been covered in preceding entries, so we will draw attention here to just two: writing frames, and reflective and analytical entries.

Writing frames are like training wheels on a bike—they provide scaffolding to support students' thinking and organization as they become more proficient in scientific writing. Common frames include: *I think that because . . . ; My results show . . . ; I observed . . . ;* and *The variable I will change is. . . .* You may be able to think of frames that best meet your content and goals. For example, if the goal is to demonstrate understanding of a particular concept the frame may be as specific as *Potential energy is important because. . . .*

Reflective and analytic writing is important in allowing students to express their own thoughts and ideas on a topic, to ask questions, and to clarify and revise their thinking. For example, after learning about DNA students might be asked to read and write about the idea of cloning and its ethical implications. They may be asked to reference their learning about DNA in their writing to justify their thinking. This type of writing may also be undertaken on an online class discussion site where students can read and react to their classmates' ideas.

Math Notebooks

There are many reasons and ways to use math notebooks. Some teachers keep interactive notebooks in which students paste or staple work they have done on teacher reproducibles, student made "foldables" (folded paper of some form with information on concepts and calculations on the inside and a title on the outside), diagrams, and writing prompts. Others may just have students do practice exercises. Some have students keep vocabulary notebooks. All of these have positive aspects. Some teachers distinguish between a notebook and a journal. The journal becomes a place for students to reflect on their learning and to practice putting knowledge into words. It provides insight for the teacher into what students understand and are struggling with, and also works as a portfolio of students' growth. Just as learning a concept in math is beyond computation, the learning can be demonstrated in many ways. However, the importance of reflection on learning is difficult to understate. Writing is one of the main ways, but not the only way, in which this learning can be demonstrated. Fletcher and Santoli (2003) describe how they did not know what their high school students had failed to understand until they asked them to write about important concepts. For example, they asked students to "describe the importance of the unit circle in trigonometry." Their students knew how to use unit circles in computation, but had difficulty writing about them.

At the risk of stating the obvious, writing about any topic in science and math may be enhanced by discussions. Graham and Hodgson (2008) describe the use of synchronous chat rooms and asynchronous discussion forums in their high school. Their goal was to encourage students to use math vocabulary to co-construct meaning. They monitored the discussions and gave credit for using specific target words. They found that "electronic communication allows non-native speakers time to plan out well-constructed responses or use others' responses as grammatical templates for their own thoughts" (p. 26). They compared the mathematical understanding of students who had been part of online discussions with those who had not, and found a positive effect on student learning.

Pass the Concept

Khoury-Bowers (2011) suggests a writing activity to review concepts that have been taught in a unit. The number of major concepts may determine group size for this activity. Each member of the group is given a different concept, and is asked to write one important idea. The concept is then passed to the next group member, who adds an additional idea. The process continues until everyone has contributed to defining the concept (or has decided that there is no new information). Groups then share their ideas for each concept with the rest of the class.

Writing for Studying

Benjamin (2011), in her book on literacy strategies for math, describes her personal use of writing for studying. An acknowledged math phobic, she studied for the Geometry Regents by doing practice problems and then writing "the explanations of my wrong answers—what I had been thinking, and what I should have been thinking" (p. xxiii). If a testimonial was needed for the power of writing, hers is a wonderfully written and powerful one, and she went on to write a book about mathematics. We need to scaffold instruction for our students that they become aware of the power of reflective writing in problem solving. Until they experience this, they will not write independently, and budding mathematicians and scientists may be lost to us.

Organizing for Discussion and Word Study

Discussion in math and science is an important component of learning. Teachers have their own preferences in how to organize their classrooms, but there are two approaches that can promote effective discussion and learning of vocabulary.

Cooperative Groups

Most literature circles or inquiry circles, where students take on particular roles in a group, have one role related to vocabulary. Shook, Hazelcorn, and Lozano (2011) describe using what they termed Collaborative Strategic Reading (CSR) in a ninth-grade biology class. Students were assigned to groups in which there was a leader, a clunk expert, and announcer, an encourager, and a reporter. Their study looked at vocabulary learning across 8 weeks and found a positive effect for CSR. The roles that are of interest to us in relation to vocabulary are:

- Clunk expert—reminds the groups of steps to follow in figuring out difficult words.
- Announcer—keeps the teacher-produced vocabulary cards and calls on members to read or share an idea when the words appear in the reading.
- Reporter—keeps track of the words students know and which they are struggling with.

As with all cooperative learning, it takes time for students to become comfortable with participating in a particular way. Shook et al. (2011) found that their ninth graders were comfortable after 3 days, and were able to engage in the process effectively for 30 minutes of two 90-minute periods a week.

Workstations

Workstations have a long history in education, but not as much in vocabulary instruction. Pries and Hughes (2012) describe how they used vocabulary workstations in their middle school classroom to introduce some vocabulary in earth science. They set up five workstations that had a set of words and some familiar objects. They provide three examples, one of which was for a unit on forces and Newton's laws. The stations had (1) spinning tops; (2) yo-yos; (3) wind-up toys; (4) a water toy; and (5) toys with wheels. The words were *contact force, gravity, friction, air resistance, tension, balanced, unbalanced, centripetal, pressure,* and *normal.* At each station students had to draw a picture of the object and use label arrows to name the forces acting on it. After completing the rotation there was some class discussion around the students' answers. The authors suggest that four components of the activity that made it successful with students: (1) not grading the answers; (2) students' limited prior knowledge of the vocabulary; (3) encouraging the students to play; and (4) using familiar objects. They argue that such workstations encourage discussion and lead to effective learning later in the units.

Concluding Thoughts

Math and science instruction is complex, but it can also be exciting and engaging. Teaching academic vocabulary in these content areas is generally thought to consist primarily of teaching the major concepts that are part of the disciplines. What we have suggested in this chapter is that it is that, but also it is more than that. There is so much academic vocabulary in these areas that it is important for us to immerse our students in a world of words, use them, write them, and have them speak and write them. It is exciting to introduce students to new ideas and new concepts, and we need to model this enthusiasm as part of our instruction.

CHAPTER 7

Resources for Developing Academic Vocabulary in Grades 6–12

In our previous chapters, we have described perspectives on academic vocabulary and given many authentic examples of classroom instruction across the disciplines. As we have developed these ideas with teachers and in classrooms, we have been asked numerous questions not only about instruction, but also about tools that can help teachers plan instruction and make learning academic vocabulary richer, deeper, and more rewarding for students. This chapter presents our answers to some of the questions we hear as we visit classrooms and collaborate with teachers who want to share ideas. These questions are as follows:

- "How can we choose words for content-area instruction?"
- "How many words should I teach?"
- "What are good resources for vocabulary instruction and learning in grades 6–12?"
- "What kind of leadership ensures vibrant vocabulary instruction in our schools?"

Choosing Words for Content-Area Instruction

Teachers know that students have a right to be instructed on key disciplinary vocabulary, but they sometimes feel unsure about selecting the most important vocabulary to teach. Beck and colleagues (2013) have been leaders in promoting the idea of three tiers of word importance. As described in earlier chapters of this book, Tier Three words are unfamiliar words for specific concepts that need extended time and effort for instruction in content-area classes; Tier Two words are those that are new labels for established concepts; and Tier One words are the most basic words that usually do not require instruction in school for students whose are comfortable with English as the language of instruction. However, given the informational demands of domain-focused learning in grades 6–12, there are other useful methodologies for selecting words for instruction.

The SWIT model, which stands for Selecting Words (from) Instructional Texts (Graves et al., 2014), suggests that teachers analyze words likely to be unfamiliar to students into four categories:

- *Essential words*, which are critical to understanding the text and its content domain.
- *Valuable words*, which may not be domain focused but which have broad, general utility for students' reading and writing, and thus have enduring importance. Many general academic terms fall into this category.
- *Accessible words*, which are more common or higher frequency words that are not likely to be understood by those students with limited vocabulary knowledge.
- *Imported words*, which are words that enhance a reader's understanding, appreciation, or learning from a text, but are not included in it.

The next step is determining the optimal method of instruction for these words. The teacher must consider how concrete or abstract the word is, knowing that abstract words take more focused instruction (Sadoski, Goetz, & Fritz, 1993; Schwanenflugel, Stahl, & McFalls, 1997), whereas concrete words may be easily taught through a synonym, picture, or other fast methodology. Words whose meanings are clearly explained by context, or that can be inferred by students, can be targets for independent instruction on inferring meaning. In all events, essential words need to be experienced in differing instructional contexts for thorough learning. Figure 7.1 shows words selected for a chapter on the Silk Road trade routes from a world history class.

It is also important to engage students in monitoring their own word learning, as we discussed in Chapter 3. The textual materials used in many classrooms can facilitate choosing domain vocabulary. Boldface, highlighting, and glossaries help with this selection process. The frequency of a term's occurrence also provides a clue to its importance, as does its use in diagrams/figures and in labeling. The CCSS highlight the need for students to develop the ability to independently monitor their own word learning in each discipline, as in the following Language Standard: "6. Acquire and use accurately general academic and domain-specific words and phrases, sufficient for reading, writing, speaking, and listening at the college and career readiness level; demonstrate independence in gathering vocabulary

Unfamiliar relevant words	Type of word			Imported	Type of instruction		
	Essential	Valuable	Accessible		Focus instruction	Fast instruction	Infer meaning
ambassador			x				
ancestor			x				x
authoritarian	x					x	
bastion		x					x
commerce	x			*commercial*	x		
Confucius				X			
construction			x				
deployed							x
dynasty	x				x		
emperor			x	*Empire*			x
export	x			*-port* words			x
philosopher		x					
sanction		x					
Silk road	x				x		
trade route	x					x	
turbulence		x					
rebellion			x				x
pretext		x			x		
precedent		x				x	
profitable	x				x		x
landlords			x			x	
provinces	X					x	
paraphrase				X			
represent				x			

FIGURE 7.1. Academic word selection grid for a chapter on the Silk Road trade routes from a world history class.

knowledge when considering a word or phrase important to comprehension or expression" (NGA & CCSSO, 2010a, p. 25).

Kayla, a reading specialist in a linguistically diverse high school, works with many discipline-area teachers in planning their units. She recommends that they use text previewing to help students learn how to monitor vocabulary for study. For example, teachers were planning an introductory freshman science career module for a unit on sound engineering. The module contained a number of book, periodical, and Web references about sound, an important background concept of the unit. The texts were on many levels and in several languages, reflecting the linguistic diversity and range of reading abilities in the class. In the module, the science teachers prepared their students for this activity by teaching a mini-lesson on typographical clues and word frequency, to help the students identify appropriate words from the books. They also introduced them to the academic vocabulary *boldface* and *frequency*. The teachers concluded the mini-lesson by stating, "You need to use *text features* to pick out important vocabulary. If a word is *boldfaced* and is *frequent*, or occurs many times, then it is probably an important word." The students' assignment was to skim their chosen book to locate three to five words that they believed would be important to the unit and should be learned. They were instructed to write these words on sticky notes to bring to the large-group discussion.

When the large group reconvened, students placed their sticky notes on the chart so that they could see the frequency of words selected, which for the most part were the most critical terms. They also explained the reasoning for their choices and revealed to the teacher other words that they thought might be "sticking points." In this way, the class constructed a chart of important terms (the most frequent words on their sticky notes). The teachers also added words they had selected as important, if the students did not contribute them to the chart.

Charlene Cobb, a district reading coordinator, supported her teachers in working together to select words across the grades and disciplines. Her method was to have each team of teachers choose 100 words for study during the year in each content area. Teachers in each discipline came together to compile a list of words from their textbooks that were identified as words for instruction. To cross check, the teachers used word lists such as those created by Coxhead (2000) for general academic vocabulary, Marzano (2004) for specific domain lists, Burke (2014) on his English composition website (*www.englishcompanion.com/pdfDocs/acvocabulary2.pdf*), as well as other Web resources (e.g., *www.myvocabulary.com/word-list/biology-vocabulary*). Teachers then worked as a team to identify the most essential words for instruction, and organized their list to match the sequence of the curriculum. This collaborative process also had an interesting effect on parents, who sometimes felt the curriculum differed dramatically from teacher to teacher. The teachers' team decision making communicated to the parents the integrity of the content-area instruction across different classrooms; it also allowed parents to know and reinforce the vocabulary at home, if and when they could.

Deciding How Many Words to Teach

The question of how many words to teach is a tricky one, with no firm answer in the research literature. Researchers on vocabulary intervention programs (Beck & McKeown, 2007; Marzano & Pickering, 2005; Snow et al., 2009) worked with a range of 100 to 250 words per year, or three to six words a week. Biemiller (2005) suggests 1,000 words per year, which works out to about 25–30 words a week, although these are words for primary students—many of these words are already found in a child's oral vocabulary. In our study of student self-selection (Fisher et al., 1991), which we discussed earlier, student groups selected more than 75 words for study for a 3-week period. And in helping us develop our process of flood, fast, and focus (described in Chapter 3), our teachers settled on 8–12 words per week as a "doable" number in a discipline, to be followed up with weekly review and assessment (Blachowicz et al., 2010). The teachers decided these should be "everybody" words—words each student needed to know.

We also need to acknowledge the differing utility of unknown words. For example, the text for a science unit on sound contains the vocabulary word *pinnae* (the visible portions of the ear that project from the head). It's a word that most adults do not know, and it does not have high utility in helping the students understand the key issues of how sound is produced. This is therefore a low-utility word, and even though it is unknown, it should not be high on the list of key vocabulary.

In that same unit, the term *vibration* is essential, as is *waveform*. Without an understanding of these two terms, the production of sound is incomprehensible. These are "everybody" words. All students need to understand these words and be able to use them in their speech, writing, and other expressive endeavors (such as lab work and lab reports) if they are to understand sound; they also need to understand the concepts of *vibration* and *waveform* in other contexts.

A third consideration in how many words to teach is how hard words are to teach. Some terms are simple synonyms for related concepts; if you have seen a wave, you can understand *waveform* without too much instruction.

We introduced you earlier to our three-word mnemonic for vocabulary teaching: *flood, fast,* and *focus.* First, *flood* your classroom with words related to your topic of study, not all of which you want your students to learn to the same depth. You want them to have seen and heard these words, such as *pinnae,* and relate them to the general topical category. They can create word blasts or semantic maps, and engage in sorting and other playful activities, to begin building a relational net of terms related to sound. You can have as many flood words as you want in a class to enrich the environment, but these are not assigned to all students or tested in traditional ways. Rather, they form a backdrop of topically related terms for incidental learning.

Use *fast* instruction for terms like *waveform*, where an easy definition or analogy will build on knowledge the students already have. Make sure the students see the word, can pronounce it, and have a "student-friendly" definition for the term. Often a visual or physical description helps as well. For students whose grade-level English vocabulary is still developing, follow up with extra practice and use.

Use *focused* instruction for words like *acoustic resonance*, where deeper, semantically rich teaching of a new concept is required. This is the type of conceptual instruction that takes time and energy, but it pays off with deep learning of those Tier Three words. If fast and focused words are "everybody" words, keep them to a reasonable number, and remember to factor in words from all your content areas to make sure that students are not overloaded. You can also pretest students on unit vocabulary and assign different lists (flood, fast, focus) to different students as needed.

Good Resources for Vocabulary Instruction in Grades 6–12

Teachers and students need good tools to help them monitor and enjoy word learning. In the last decade, there has been an explosion in good reference tools for grades 6–12. In this section, we describe basic references—dictionaries, encyclopedias, and thesauruses—in both book and online formats, as well as word games, software, and other resources.

Learner Dictionaries

There are many lists of good dictionaries for our target-age students (Blachowicz & Fisher, 2014), but so many times these are not helpful because the definitions are too complex for developing readers. We have found that all students benefit from access to what are called *learner dictionaries*. These are reference tools with definitions written in clear and "student-friendly" ways—that is, with language that can be easily understood and with salient examples.

Excellent examples of learner dictionaries are the Longman Learner Dictionaries, whose clear, easily understood definitions provide access to the basic vocabulary that underpins more complex content learning. These are available at various levels, and audio CDs are also available for some of them.

Basic/Beginning

Longman Photo Dictionary of American English. Designed for adult learners of English, this new dictionary uses clear, contemporary color photos to make new words easy to remember. Suitable for both classroom and home use, this dictionary teaches real-world language in realistic contexts to help beginners master more than 3,000 key words.

Low Beginning–Low Intermediate

Longman Basic Dictionary of American English. The clear, simple definitions in this dictionary are written with the 2,000-word *Longman Defining Vocabulary*, which means that students are sure to understand the explanations. Helpful, natural examples illustrate the words and phrases in typical contexts, so students learn as well as understand. The engaging cartoons and clear, open design contribute to a dictionary that students will enjoy using.

Beginning/Low Intermediate—Intermediate

Longman Study Dictionary of American English. This new dictionary is guaranteed to help students understand difficult words and concepts, many of which are found in content-area classes. Again, every definition is written with the *Longman Defining Vocabulary* of the 2,000 most common words. The examples provide further explanation of the definitions, to be sure students understand and can differentiate words in the same family.

Low Intermediate

Longman Dictionary of American English, Fourth Edition. The most recent edition of this well-regarded American English learner dictionary helps intermediate students build their vocabulary. It now offers extra help and support for students who are studying other subjects in English.

Beginning—High Intermediate

Longman American Idioms Dictionary. Help your students "get a handle" on all kinds of American idioms with this dictionary, which contains more than 4,000 idioms from spoken and written English. Again, these are defined with the 2,000-word *Longman Defining Vocabulary.*

Intermediate—Advanced

There are many other Longman Learners Dictionaries in dual languages and at differing levels of complexity (available at *www.pearsonlongman.com/ae/ dictionaries/content.html*).

Standard Vocabulary References

Conventional School Dictionaries and Thesauruses

For Upper Elementary/Junior High School

Webster's Thesaurus for Students, Third Edition

For High School

English Vocabulary Quick Reference: A Dictionary Arranged by Word Roots (Lexadyne)

Merriam-Webster Online: Dictionary and Thesaurus (www.merriam-webster. com)

Scribner-Bantam English Dictionary

Webster's New World Dictionary

Webster's New World Thesaurus

Online Dictionaries

For many students and teachers, online dictionaries are the references of choice. Dictionary.com (*www.dictionary.com*) is the "granddaddy" of electronic resources. Other electronic tools include the following:

Word Central Merriam-Webster (*www.wordcentral.com*). Dictionary, thesaurus, and rhyming dictionary plus games for educators; now reprogrammed for superior word power and language fun.

English Pronouncing Dictionary with Instant Sound (*www.howjsay.com*). Here is a neat dictionary that says the word for your students! They will really like this. Well-read persons know hundreds, even thousands, of words that they've never heard anyone pronounce. Search through the 82,576 sound files and listen while somebody pronounces your chosen mystery words.

Merriam-Webster Visual Dictionary (*http://visual.merriam-webster.com*). This visual dictionary will help your students translate words into pictures. You can browse by broad themes (animal kingdom, food and kitchen, arts and architecture, science, sports and games, etc.). The search engine takes some getting used to—enter your word, wait for the word to display under "Images," click on it, and hit "Go to." When the image (or images) is displayed, its theme is highlighted on the navigation bar. Sometimes detailed images that *are* there (e.g., a pommel horse) won't show up in a search but can be accessed through the broader category they're part of (in the case of the pommel horse, gymnastics).

Acronymfinder (*www.acronymfinder.com*). Determine the meaning of acronyms. We are surrounded by acronyms, especially in the areas of science and economics (as well as in education!). This resource can help clarify this confusing alphabet soup.

Roget's Thesaurus (*www.thesaurus.com*). This is a classic for unraveling closely related terms and is a writer's aid as well.

Merriam-Webster Dictionary HD. Offers voice search without having to spell a word, along with synonyms, antonyms, and example sentence. All ages.

Your Dictionary (*www.yourdictionary.com*). Within this accessible online dictionary, students can browse existing words and word lists, or they can develop their own lists. From these lists, flashcards and other study tools can be generated.

Visuwords Online Graphical Dictionary (*www.viswords.com*). This fun online dictionary generates colorful, moving semantic maps of a target word's meaning, associations to other words or concepts, synonyms, and antonyms.

Domain-Specific References

There are also many dictionaries available for school use that focus on the content areas. The Usborne Content Dictionaries (*www.usborne.com*) are also learner dictionaries because of their clear, friendly definitions, as well as examples and graphics that deal with math, science, history, music, and other content domains.

For disciplinary vocabulary, encyclopedias are often the best resources because they provide the extended context required to understand such vocabulary. Though good encyclopedias often come bundled in school computer packages, the following are also highly regarded:

DK E-Encyclopedia (*www.dke-encyc.com/youandinternet.asp*). Dorling Kindersley and Google bring you their best of the Web. Dorling Kindersley is known for providing excellent photographs and diagrams that explicate concepts clearly.

Columbia Encyclopedia (*http://education.yahoo.com/reference/encyclopedia*). This free online encyclopedia contains over 50,000 entries and more than 84,000 hypertext cross-references, covering a wide range of research and reference topics. The Columbia Encyclopedia is one of the most complete and up-to-date electronic encyclopedias ever produced.

Many online dictionaries have the advantage of combining an invaluable research tool with exhaustive information, ranging from the general purpose *Oxford Pocket Dictionary of Current English,* to social science terms in *A Dictionary of Psychology,* to health-related nutrition definitions in *A Dictionary of Food Nutrition.*

Roots and affixes are important tools for understanding words. References focusing on morphology include the following:

For affixes: One Look (*www.onelook.com*). Students can look up examples in which prefixes, suffixes, and roots are used. An asterisk (*) allows for "wild card" searches. Thus *ion searches for all words with the *-ion* suffix, while micro* searches for all words with the *micro* prefix.

For word roots: Word Info (*http://wordinfo.info*). Explains the meaning of roots, including Greek and Latin clustering.

Other useful discipline-specific resources include:

For chemistry vocabulary definitions: *www.csun.edu/science/books/source-book/chapters/1-vocabulary/resources/chemistry_roots.pdf*

For biology terms: *www.biology-online.org/dictionary/Main_Page*

For physics terms: e-Tutor physics glossary of terms (*www.etutorphysics.com/glossary.html*)

For history: Babylon history dictionary (*www.babylon.com/define/24/History-Dictionary.html*). Babylon has many other domain dictionaries.

For American history: Course Notes Dictionary of American History (*www.course-notes.org/us_history/vocabulary_terms*). Course Notes offers online references for many typical high school course offerings.

Specialized Dictionaries and Encyclopedias

Who2 (*www.who2.com*). Who2 is an encyclopedia of famous people. It includes well-researched profiles of real people, fictional characters, and some figures (like Robin Hood) who may be either. It also includes profiles of celebrities who aren't people, like Ham the Chimp and Hal 9000.

Encyclopedia of Greek and Roman Mythology (Roman & Roman, 2010). This is a comprehensive and sophisticated compendium of Greek and Roman mythology, for *The Lightning Thief* mavens and other lovers of ancient myths.

The Cook's Thesaurus (*www.foodsubs.com*). The Cook's Thesaurus is actually a cooking encyclopedia that covers thousands of ingredients and kitchen tools. Entries include pictures, descriptions, synonyms, pronunciations, and suggested substitutions.

So many specialized content dictionaries and encyclopedias, both in book form and online, cover topics of personal interest to students. One high school English teacher, Alex, who also loves technology, assigns students the task of locating these resources as new ones arrive every day. This is also a way for Alex to get to know his students' interests and strengths.

Games and Other Resources for Developing Vocabulary

Vocabulary Games and Gamefication

We have long suggested that we need to put the *fun* back in the *fundamentals*, and this is certainly true of vocabulary instruction (Blachowicz & Fisher, 2012). *Gamefication* is a term used by educational technology designers to refer to the modification of educational design to include gaming (Zeichermann & Cunningham, 2011). Incorporating gaming strategies into the middle and secondary curricula is a topic of major interest in instructional design and a "natural" approach for older learners (Abrams & Walsh, 2014). Games and play, in general, are also avenues for academic vocabulary learning.

Domain Vocabulary Games

Dr. Norman Herr's Source Book for Teaching Science. This book for grades 6–12 by Dr. Norman Herr (2008) has many super ideas for vocabulary activities and games for secondary science.

The website *www.csun.edu/science/ref/games* adapts games we all know, like Pictionary. For example, can you guess this botany term?

[The answer is *photosynthesis*.]

www.MyVocabulary.com. Games and puzzles for high school science, math and history.

www.digitaldialects.com. Games for Italian, French, German, and other languages.

Crossword Puzzle Tool (*www.readwritethink.org/files/resources/interactives/crossword/crossword.swf*). Students and teachers love this tool, which allows them to create wonderful puzzles from their academic vocabulary.

General Vocabulary Games

Building word interest and consciousness is aided by having good word games in the classroom. Old favorites, like Scrabble, Spill and Spell, and Boggle (see the list below), can help build a "game library" for your classroom or school, and most are available in online versions. Some schools keep sets of games in the school library to circulate among classes. Games for the classroom might include the following:

Apples to Apples. Players will delight in all the crazy comparisons, while expanding their vocabulary and thinking skills at the same time. Grade 6 and up. Mattel.

Bananagrams. Players race against each other to build crossword grids and use all their letter tiles first. All ages. Banangrams.

Blurt!: The Webster's Game of Word Racing. Players take turns reading a definition aloud while others blurt out guesses in a race for the right word. Age 10–adult; travel version available. Riverside Publishing Company.

Boggle—Players associate words with pictures and find letters on cubes that match the letters in the words. All ages. Parker Brothers.

Boggle Master: 3-Minute Word Game. Players link letters up, down, sideways, and diagonally to form words within the time limit. Age 8–adult. Parker Brothers.

Buzz Word. Teams have 45 seconds to solve 10 clues to name words that contain the "buzz" word—for example, *ball* in *ballroom*. Age 10 and up. Patch Products.

Claymania. Players draw cards with words that depict the object into which the clay must be molded within the 45-second time limit. Age 12 and up. Gamewright.

Don't Say It. Can you get your team to say *pig* without using the words *sausage, bacon, sty,* or *pork*? You'll need to be quick to avoid being buzzed out by the timer. All ages. Pressman Toy.

Go to the Head of the Class (Deluxe Edition). Players answer quiz questions that are divided into three knowledge levels and cover every subject. Age 8–adult. Milton Bradley.

Guesstures: The Game of Split-Second Charades. Players act out four words at a time within a given time limit. Age 8–adult. Milton Bradley.

Last Word. Players name members of a category that begin with the same letter in a given time period. All ages. Buffalo Games.

Lexogon One. Players think of words of four or more letters that use their two "clue" letters in a particular way. Age 9–adult. Tippecanoe Games.

Outburst. Players on a team have 60 seconds to yell out answers that fit familiar categories within a given time limit. Age 12–adult. Parker Brothers.

Pictionary: The Classic Game of Quick Draw for Kids. Players sketch clues for teammates, who have to quickly guess the word from the card that was drawn. Age 12–adult. Pictionary.

Quiddler. Letter cards are arranged into increasingly longer words. Rules can be adapted for younger players. All ages. SET Enterprises.

Scrabble Crossword Game. Players connect letter titles up and down and across the board to make words of various point values. Age 8–adult. Milton Bradley.

TriBond Riddle Game. "The fun starts with 3 seemingly unrelated clues. What do a violinist, an archer, and a fancy gift have in common? You win the card if your team guesses, 'They all have bows.'" Age 10–15. TriBond Enterprises.

Online Word Web and Word Cloud Generators

As we discussed in Chapter 3, generating one's own word web or word cloud can be an engaging activity. Luckily, many resources exist online to make this an easy process to produce very professional looking products. Some websites to try include the following:

www.lucidchart.com
bubbl.us
www.spicynodes.org
Word Mosaic (*www.imagechef.com/ic/word_mosaic*)
Wordle.com
Visual Thesaurus: Vocab Grabber (*www.visualthesaurus.com/vocabgrabber*) is a real favorite for creating a visual representation of words. Teachers and students can paste any text into Vocab Grabber, and the site automatically generates a list of the most useful vocabulary words within that text. Words are categorized by subject area (e.g., geography, social studies, people, science), and students can click on a subject to see all the words in the text that fit into a given category. When students click on a word, a visual thesaurus representation is generated based on similar words within the text.

The following is a selective list of the many other online games available. Ask your students to do a search and share their favorites with the class.

spellingcity.com. Twenty-five games with over 42,000 words, to play online or print, including parts of speech and vocabulary test. Kindergarten to high school.

Spelling City App. Same games available online can also be played on app. Can choose own words to practice. Kindergarten through high school.

vocabulary.co.il. Games to enhance vocabulary and practice skills. Kindergarten to high school.

Enchanted Dictionary 7–12th Grade. Helps students learn core vocabulary for science, social studies, math, or ELA. Select the words you wish to practice and press play.

Vocabology. View word of the day from several sources on the Internet. Test your knowledge with a quiz game that tests you with the words you've seen. Junior high and up.

Vocabulary Central Grade 6, 7, 8, 9, 10, 11, or 12. This app offers support activities such as interactive flashcards, songs, and trivia games. Sixth grade and up.

Word-Detective.com. Online version of The Word Detective, a newspaper column answering readers' questions about words and language.

World Wide Words (*www.worldwidewords.org*). Each week you will find at least one short article or extended definition of a word that is too new to appear in most dictionaries.

Imangi. This free iPad app is a cross between Scrabble, Boggle, and Rubiks Cube. Players create as many words as they can by rearranging letters on the screen.

Quizlet. This website and accompanying notebook/smartphone app allows students and teachers to create online flashcards and study guides. Users also have access to 50+ million existing flash card sets on a variety of topics.

Software

Billiards 'n' Antonyms. Heartsoft. (third to eighth grade)

Billiards 'n' Homonyms. Heartsoft. (third to eighth grade)

Billiards 'n' Synonyms. Heartsoft. (third to eighth grade)

Crossword Weaver. Variety Games Inc. (teachers)

Kaplan: Writing and Vocabulary Essential Review. Encore Software. (high school)

Letter Rack. SoftSpot Software. (sixth grade and up)

Spinner's Choice. Heartsoft. (third to eighth grade)

Super Tutor Vocabulary. HomeworkHelp. (seventh to 12th grade)

Word Foundry. Nordic Software. (second grade to adult)

Word Ladder. DLK Quality Educational Software. (third grade and up)

Words Rock. EdAlive. (kindergarten to ninth grade)

Books for Older Students for Expanding Vocabulary and Wordplay

Albert, J. (2010). *Black sheep and lame ducks: The origins of even more phrases we use every day.* New York: Perigee Trade. (ninth grade and up)

Bowler, P. (2001). *The superior person's book of words.* New York: Laurel. (sixth grade and up)

Crystal, D. (2007). *Words, words, words.* New York: Oxford University Press. Kindle edition available. (ninth grade and up)

Cutler, C. (2000). *O brave new words: Native American loanwords in current English.* Norman: University of Oklahoma Press. (sixth grade and up)

Dubosarsky, U. (2009). *The word snoop.* New York: Dial. (fifth to ninth grade)

Editors of the American heritage dictionaries. (2004). *Word histories and mysteries: From abracadabra to Zeus.* Orlando: Houghton Mifflin Harcourt. (ninth grade and up)

Elster, C. H. (2005). *What in the word? Wordplay, word lore, and answers to your peskiest questions about language.* Fort Washington, PA: Harvest Books. (sixth grade and up)

Funk, C. E. (2002). *Horsefeathers and other curious words.* New York: Collins. (sixth grade and up)

Funk, C. E. (2007). *Thereby hangs a tale—stories of curious word origins.* New York: Collins. Kindle edition available. (ninth grade and up)

Garg, A. (2007). *The dord, the diglot, and an avocado or two: The hidden lives and strange origins of common and not-so-common words.* New York: Plume. Only Kindle edition available. (sixth grade and up)

Grambs, D. (1997). *The endangered English dictionary: Bodacious words your dictionary forgot.* New York: Norton. (sixth grade and up)

Grothe, M. (2004). *Oxymoronica: Paradoxical wit and wisdom from history's greatest wordsmiths.* New York: Collins. Kindle edition available. (ninth grade and up)

Hole, G. (2005). *The real McCoy: Why we say the things we say.* New York: Oxford University Press. (sixth grade and up)

Jack, A. (2005). *Red herrings and white elephants: The origins of the phrases we use every day.* New York: HarperCollins. Kindle edition available. (sixth grade and up)

Schur, N. (1982). *1,000 most important words.* New York: Ballantine. (ninth grade and up)

Smitherman-Donaldson, G. (1994). *Black talk: Words and phrases from the hood to the amen corner.* Boston: Houghton Mifflin. (sixth grade and up)

Umstatter, J. (2002). *Where words come from.* London: Franklin Watts. (fourth to eighth grade)

Leadership for Academic Vocabulary Development

All of the resources and approaches described above are effective tools when used by knowledgeable teachers in schools where there is leadership for academic vocabulary learning. Leadership is required in the district, in the school, and in the classroom. Let's look at how three professionals who work in multicultural metropolitan districts describe what's important in their educational settings.

At the District Level

Charlene Cobb is Assistant Superintendent for Teaching and Learning who is responsible for curriculum and instruction for grades K–12. In her view, leadership for academic vocabulary learning has to be established at all levels, but the district-level leadership is responsible for setting district expectations for administrators. She comments:

> "The most important thing a literacy director can do to provide leadership and to stimulate the teaching and learning of academic vocabulary in a district is understand the underlying needs and work with the principals to support the needs of the students and teachers. Needs are determined by examining various sources of data and understanding the school cultures related to instruction. From this, the literacy director needs to formulate goals and action plans that can be shared with principals. I have found that principal support is critical to effectively working with teachers to support students. Getting principal buy-in is critical. The next step is providing principals with the knowledge needed to support the goals. Sometimes this can be as simple as a phone call or meeting, and other times it might mean providing presentations, discussing articles, doing a book study, or giving principals an article/book to read on their own.
>
> "The most important things a principal can do to provide leadership and to stimulate the teaching and learning of academic vocabulary in a school are very similar to what a literacy leader does in terms of understanding the underlying need. However, in order to determine need, they first need an understanding of best practices for academic vocabulary and access to resources. I've found that some principals do this almost organically; others seek the support of their reading specialists or coaches; and some search for programs that will 'fix' the problem. The most powerful instances I've witnessed are when principals and teachers meet on a regular basis for professional discourse around questions such as these: What are our students' needs? What do we need to do in order to meet these needs? How will we know when we've done this? What is our plan? How will we implement and monitor this plan? These are simple sentences that lead to complex conversations."

At the School Level

Ellen Fogelberg is a master staff developer and a former superintendent for curriculum. Ellen agrees with Char's points above and adds these tips for principals:

- "Make vocabulary a school priority, and support innovative, motivational, and fun ways to build your 'brand' as a vocabulary school."
- "Make sure that your professional development is sustained long enough to make a difference. Research by the National Staff Development Council [Darling-Hammond, Wei, Andree, Richardson, & Orphanos, 2009] suggests [that] at least 60 hours of professional development [are] needed to effect change."
- "Organize the schedule so teachers have time to meet in grade and departmental groups and cross-grade groups for school articulation."
- "Provide support personnel to work with teachers and encourage teachers to collaborate for mutual support, emphasizing that instructional leadership is distributed across the school."
- "Administrators should participate in teacher work groups, and work with support personnel to monitor and support group ideas."
- "Provide the resources teachers need to do a good job."
- "Connect with other principals to share concerns, issues, and ideas."
- "Spotlight the good news about vocabulary instruction in your school to parents and the wider community."

At the Classroom Level

Connie Obrochta is a teacher leader and literacy coach in a large multicultural school. She works with teachers and children to actualize instruction in the classroom.

Connie reflects on what is needed for teacher leadership at the classroom level:

"I think it's important that the PD [professional development] for the teachers is manageable and sustained, so they are taking this work to a deeper level over time through a scaffolded approach. In order for the PD to truly 'take root' and make an impact on student achievement, it's important to develop and sustain a school culture where all teachers in the building are encouraged and expected to (1) regularly observe and describe their students' strengths and needs; (2) discuss and design instruction based upon those needs; and (3) regularly share with colleagues in grade-level teams and across grade levels what they have learned and what they are thinking about for next steps. I think if those systems aren't in place, there will be some strong examples happening in individual classrooms, but the power of having the whole school/district moving in a seamless direction for the children will likely be diluted.

"I've come to believe that principals are the most critical component in crafting this kind of culture over time. Their presence during instructional team conversations can make or break the sustainability of this work."

At the middle and secondary levels, it is particularly important that literacy coaches probe for and listen to the vocabulary and language challenges that disciplinary teachers encounter. While literacy coaches might not be experts within those language domains, they can seek out resources to support and address the challenges that teachers articulate. As we've discussed in preceding chapters, different content areas do require different approaches to language and vocabulary learning. While there are certainly strategies that can be used across disciplines, such as a Knowledge Rating, no single approach fits all and will be able to address the unique, domain-specific language and vocabulary demands that older students face.

Teacher Study Groups

Teachers in schools with effective academic vocabulary programs take their leadership roles seriously. At schools in these districts, teachers often form their own study groups to work on issues, to review the latest research and practice literature, to try out ideas in the classroom, and to reflect with one another on student performance. These are "growth groups" where they can take chances, exchange ideas, and build their capacity to lead in the classroom and in the school. There are many resources for teacher study groups in vocabulary, and several books are devoted to setting up such groups (see Figure 7.2).

A survey of more than 200 teachers attending local meetings of the International Reading Association identified the books listed in Figure 7.3 (two of which

---

- Cayuso, E., Fegan, C., & McAlister, D. (2004). *Designing teacher study groups: A guide for success.* Gainesville, FL: Maupin House.
- Dimino, J., & Taylor, M. (2009). *Learning how to improve vocabulary instruction through teacher study groups.* Baltimore, MD: Brookes.
- Murphy, C., & Lick, D. (2005). *Whole-faculty study groups: Creating professional learning communities that target student learning* (3rd ed.). Thousand Oaks, CA: Corwin Press.
- Ogle, D. (2007). *Coming together as readers* (2nd ed.). Thousand Oaks, CA: Corwin Press.

FIGURE 7.2. Resources for teacher study groups in vocabulary.

- Allen, J. (1999). *Words, words, words: Teaching vocabulary in grades 4–12*. York, ME: Stenhouse.
- Beck, I. L., McKeown, M. G., & Kucan, L. (2013). *Bringing words to life: Robust vocabulary instruction* (2nd ed.). New York: Guilford Press.
- Blachowicz, C. L. Z., & Fisher, P. (2014). *Teaching vocabulary in all classrooms* (5th ed.). Boston: Pearson/Allyn & Bacon.
- Farstrup, A., & Samuels, S. J. (Eds.). (2008). *What the research has to say about vocabulary instruction*. Newark, DE: International Reading Association.
- Ganske, K. (2014). *Word journeys: Assessment-guided phonics, spelling, and vocabulary instruction* (2nd ed.). New York: Guilford Press.
- Graves, M. F. (2006). *The vocabulary book: Learning and instruction*. New York: Teachers College Press.
- Graves, M. F. (Ed.). (2009). *Essential readings on vocabulary instruction*. Newark, DE: International Reading Association.
- Kame'enui, E. J., & Baumann, J. F. (Eds.). (2012). *Vocabulary instruction: Research to practice* (2nd ed.). New York: Guilford Press.

FIGURE 7.3. Teacher-identified core titles for study groups in vocabulary.

have been updated to reflect more recent editions) as useful core titles for study groups in vocabulary.

Concluding Thoughts

In this chapter, we have shared with you our answers to the most common questions that we have encountered in our work in schools and classrooms. Teachers have asked for guidance about selecting and prioritizing vocabulary for disciplinary instruction. They have also sought resources to make their instruction more engaging and relevant to students of a new millennium who are comfortable with technology in their daily lives. And we have shared our perspectives, and perspectives from the field, on the leadership needed to support teachers in their goal of making every student a capable and independent word learner and word lover across all areas of the curriculum.

References

Abrams, S. A., & Walsh, S. (2014). Gamified vocabulary: Online resources and enriched language learning. *Journal of Adolescent and Adult Literacy, 58*(1), 49–58.

Achugar, M., Schleppegrell, M., & Oteiza, T. (2007). Engaging teachers in language analysis: A functional linguistics approach to reflective literacy. *English Teaching: Practice and Critique, 6*(2), 8–24.

Alexie, S. (2007). *The absolutely true diary of a part-time Indian*. New York: Little, Brown.

Allen, J. (2000). *Yellow brick roads: Shared and guided paths to independent reading*. Portland, ME: Stenhouse.

Alvermann, D. (1991). The discussion web: A graphic aid for learning across the curriculum. *The Reading Teacher, 45*(2), 92–99.

Alvermann, D. E., & Hynd, C. R. (1989). Study strategies for correcting misconceptions in physics: An intervention. In S. McCormick & J. Zutell (Eds.), *Cognitive and social perspectives for literacy research and instruction: 38th Yearbook of the National Reading Conference* (pp. 353–361). Chicago: National Reading Conference.

Anderson, L. W., & Krathwohl, D. R. (Eds.). (2001). *A taxonomy for learning, teaching and assessing: A revision of Bloom's taxonomy of educational objectives: Complete edition*. New York: Longman.

Anderson, R. C., & Nagy, W. E. (1991). Word meanings. In R. Barr, M. Kamil, P. B. Mosenthal, & P. D. Pearson (Eds.), *Handbook of reading research* (Vol. 2, pp. 690–724). New York: Longman.

August, D., & Gray, J. L. (2010). Developing comprehension in English language learners. In K. Ganske & D. Fisher (Eds.), *Comprehension across the curriculum: Perspectives and practices K–12* (pp. 225–245). New York: Guilford Press.

Aukerman, M. (2007). A culpable CALP: Rethinking the conversational/academic language proficiency distinction in early literacy instruction. *The Reading Teacher, 60*, 626–634.

Bailey, A. L., Butler, F. A., LaFramenta, C., & Ong, C. (2004). *Towards the characterization of academic language in upper elementary science classrooms* (Center for the Study of Evaluation Report No. 621). Los Angeles: Graduate School of Education and Information Studies, University of California, Los Angeles.

Baker, E. A. (Ed.). (2010). *The new literacies: Multiple perspectives on research and practice*. New York: Guilford Press.

Baker, J. (2008). Trilingualism. In L. Delpit & J. K. Dowdy (Eds.), *The skin we speak: Thoughts on language and culture in the classroom* (pp. 51–61). New York: New Press.

Barr, R., Kamil, M., Mosenthal, P., & Pearson, P. D. (Eds.). (1991). *Handbook of reading research* (Vol. 2). New York: Longman.

Baumann, J. F. (2009). Intensity in vocabulary instruction and effects on reading comprehension. *Topics in Language Disorders, 29,* 312–328.

Baumann, J. F., Edwards, E. C., Boland, E., & Font, G. (2012). Teaching word learning strategies. In E. J. Kame'enui & J. F. Baumann (Eds.), *Vocabulary instruction: Research to practice* (pp. 139–166). New York: Guilford Press.

Baumann, J. F., Edwards, E. C., Boland, E., Olejnik, S., & Kame'enui, E. W. (2003). Vocabulary tricks: Effects of instruction in morphology and context on fifth-grade students' ability to derive and infer word meanings. *American Educational Research Journal, 40,* 447–494.

Baumann, J. F., & Graves, M. F. (2010). What is academic vocabulary? *Journal of Adolescent and Adult Literacy, 54*(1), 4–12.

Baumann, J. F., Kame'enui, E. J., & Ash, G. E. (2003). Research on vocabulary instruction: Voltaire redux. In J. Flood, D. Lapp, J. R. Squire, & J. M. Jensen (Eds.), *Handbook of research on teaching the English language arts* (2nd ed., pp. 752–785). Mahwah, NJ: Erlbaum.

Baumann, J. F., Manyak, P. C., Peterson, H., Blachowicz, C. L. Z., Cieply, C., Bates, A., et al. (2011, December). *Windows on formative/design-based research on vocabulary instruction: Findings and methodological challenges.* Symposium conducted at the 61st annual conference of the Literacy Research Association, Jacksonville, FL.

Baumann, J. F., Ware, D., & Edwards, E. C. (2007). "Bumping into spicy, tasty words that catch your tongue": A formative experiment on vocabulary instruction. *The Reading Teacher, 62,* 108–122.

Beck, I. L., & McKeown, M. G. (1991). Conditions of vocabulary acquisition. In R. Barr, M. Kamil, P. Mosenthal, & P. D. Pearson (Eds.), *Handbook of reading research* (Vol. 2, pp. 789–814). New York: Longman.

Beck, I. L., & McKeown, M. G. (2007). Increasing young low-income children's oral vocabulary repertoires through rich and focused instruction. *The Elementary School Journal, 107,* 251–271.

Beck, I. L., McKeown, M. G., & Kucan, L. (2013). *Bringing words to life: Robust vocabulary instruction* (2nd ed.). New York: Guilford Press.

Becker, W. C. (1977). Teaching reading and language to the disadvantaged—What we have learned from field research. *Harvard Educational Review, 47,* 518–543.

Bednarz, S., Clinton, C., Hartoonian, M., Hernandez, A., Marshall, P. L., & Nickell, P. (2003). *Discover our heritage.* Boston: Houghton Mifflin.

Benjamin, A. (2011). *Math in plain English: Literacy strategies for the mathematics classroom.* Larchmont, NY: Eye on Education.

Bergelson, E., & Swingley, D. (2013). The acquisition of abstract words by young infants. *Cognition, 127,* 391–397.

Berthoff, A. B. (1981). *The making of meaning, metaphors, models and maxims for writing teachers.* Portsmouth, NH: Heinemann.

Biemiller, A. (2005). Size and sequence in vocabulary development: Implications for choosing words for primary grade vocabulary instruction. In E. H. Hiebert & M. Kamil (Eds.), *Teaching and learning vocabulary: Bringing research to practice* (pp. 223–242). Mahwah, NJ: Erlbaum.

Biemiller, A., & Slonim, N. (2001). Estimating root word vocabulary growth in normative and advantaged populations: Evidence for a common sequence of vocabulary acquisition. *Journal of Educational Psychology, 93,* 498–520.

Bierwisch, M. (Ed.). (1983). *Pronominal reference: Child language and the theory of grammar.* Dordrecht, Holland: D. Reide.

Blachowicz, C. L. Z. (1987). Vocabulary instruction: What goes on in the classroom? *The Reading Teacher, 42*, 132–137.

Blachowicz, C. L. Z., Bates, A., & Cieply, C. (2011, May). Vocabulary framing. In C. L. Z. Blachowicz, J. F. Baumann, P. C. Manyak, A. Bates, & C. Cieply, *Boost vocabulary power in classrooms.* Symposium presented at the 56th annual convention of the International Reading Association, Orlando, FL.

Blachowicz, C. L. Z., & Baumann, J. F. (2013). Language standards for vocabulary. In L. M. Morrow, K. K. Wixson, & T. Shanahan (Eds.), *Teaching with the Common Core Standards for English language arts, grades 3–5* (pp. 131–153). New York: Guilford Press.

Blachowicz, C. L. Z., & Cobb, C. (2007). *Action tools: Vocabulary across the content areas.* Alexandria, VA: Association for Supervision and Curriculum Development.

Blachowicz, C. L. Z., & Fisher, P. (2000). Vocabulary instruction. In M. L. Kamil, P. B. Mosenthal, P. D. Pearson, & R. Barr (Eds.), *Handbook of reading research* (Vol. 3, pp. 503–523). Mahwah, NJ: Erlbaum.

Blachowicz, C. L. Z., & Fisher, P. (2004). Vocabulary lessons. *Educational Leadership, 61*(6), 66–69.

Blachowicz, C. L. Z., & Fisher, P. (2012). Keep the "fun" in *fun*damental: Encouraging word consciousness and incidental word learning in the classroom through wordplay. In E. Kame'enui & J. Baumann (Eds.), *Vocabulary instruction: Research to practice* (2nd ed., pp. 189–209). New York: Guilford Press.

Blachowicz, C. L. Z., & Fisher, P. (2014). *Teaching vocabulary in all classrooms* (5th ed.). Boston: Pearson/Allyn & Bacon.

Blachowicz, C. L. Z., Fisher, P. J. L., Ogle, D., & Watts Taffe, S. (2006). Vocabulary: Questions from the classroom. *Reading Research Quarterly, 41*, 524–539.

Blachowicz, C. L. Z., Fisher, P. J. L., Ogle, D., & Watts Taffe, S. (2013). *Teaching academic vocabulary K–8: Effective practices across the curriculum.* New York: Guilford Press.

Blachowicz, C. L. Z., & Obrochta, C. (2005). Vocabulary visits: Developing primary content vocabulary. *The Reading Teacher, 59*(3), 262–269.

Bloom, B. (1956). *Taxonomy of educational objectives: The classification of educational goals.* New York: Longman.

Braun, P. (2010). Taking the time to read aloud. *Science Scope, 34*(2), 45–49.

Britton, J. N. (1993). *Language and learning: The importance of speech in children's development* (2nd ed.). Portsmouth, NH: Heinemann.

Buehl, D. (2011). *Developing readers in the academic disciplines.* Newark, DE: International Reading Association.

Bus, A. G., van IJzendoorn, M. H., & Pellegrini, A. D. (1995). Joint book reading makes for success in learning to read: A meta-analysis on intergenerational transmission of literacy. *Review of Educational Research, 65*, 1–21.

Butler, F. A., Bailey, A. L., Stevens, R., & Huang, B. (2004). *Academic English in fifth-grade mathematics, science, and social studies textbooks* (Center for the Study of Evaluation Report No. 642). Los Angeles: Graduate School of Education and Information Studies, University of California, Los Angeles.

Carr, N. (2008). Is Google making us stupid? *The Atlantic.* Retrieved August 1, 2014, from *www.theatlantic.com/magazine/archive/2008/07/is-google-making-us-stupid/306868.*

Carrier, K. A., & Tatum, A. W. (2006). Creating sentence walls to help English-language learners develop content literacy. *The Reading Teacher, 60*, 285–288.

Chamot, A. U., & O'Malley, M. J. (1994). *CALLA handbook: Implementing the cognitive academic language learning approach.* Reading, MA: Addison-Wesley.

Coleman, R., & Goldenberg, C. (2010). What does research say about effective practice for English learners? *Kappa Delta Pi Record, 46*(2), 60–65.

Collins, S. (2008). *The hunger games.* New York: Scholastic Press.

Common Sense Media. (2014). *Children, teens and reading: A Common Sense Media research brief.* Retrieved April 1, 2015, from *www.commonsensemedia.org/research/children-teens-and-reading.*

Countryman, J. (1992). *Writing to learn mathematics: Strategies that work, K–12.* Portsmouth, NH: Heinemann.

Coxhead, A. (2000). A new academic word list. *TESOL Quarterly, 34*(2), 213–238.

Cummins, J. (2000). *Language, power and pedagogy: Bilingual children in the crossfire.* Buffalo, NY: Multilingual Matters.

Cunningham, A. E. (2005). Vocabulary growth through independent reading and reading aloud to children. In E. H. Hiebert & M. L. Kamil (Eds.), *Teaching and learning vocabulary: Bringing research to practice* (pp. 45–68). Mahwah, NJ: Erlbaum.

Cunningham, A. E., & Stanovich, K. E. (1998). What reading does for the mind. *American Educator, 22,* 8–15.

Cunningham, P. M. (2012). *Phonics they use: Words for reading and writing.* Boston: Allyn & Bacon.

Dale, E., & O'Rourke, J. P. (1976). *The living word vocabulary.* Chicago: Field Enterprises.

Darling-Hammond, L., Wei, R. C., Andree, A., Richardson, N., & Orphanos, S. (2009). *Professional learning in the learning professions: A status report on teacher development in the United States and abroad.* Palo Alto, CA: School Redesign Network.

D'Anna, C. A., Zechmeister, E. B., & Hall, J. W. (1991). Toward a meaningful definition of vocabulary size. *Journal of Reading Behavior, 23,* 109–122.

DeLuca, E. (2010). Unlocking academic vocabulary: Lessons from an ESOL teacher. *Science Teacher, 77*(3), 27–32.

Dickinson, D. K., & Smith, M. W. (1994). Long-term effects of preschool teachers' book readings on low-income children's vocabulary and story comprehension. *Reading Research Quarterly, 29,* 104–122.

Dimino, J., & Taylor, M. J. (2009). *Learning how to improve vocabulary instruction through teacher study groups.* Baltimore, MD: Brookes.

Donnelly, W. B., & Roe, C. J. (2010). Using sentence frames to develop academic vocabulary for English learners. *The Reading Teacher, 64,* 131–136.

Echevarria, J., Vogt, M. E., & Short, K. (2013). *Making content comprehensible for secondary English learners: The SIOP model* (4th ed.). Boston: Pearson.

Elleman, A. M., Endia, J. L., Morphy, P., & Compton, D. L. (2009). The impact of vocabulary instruction on passage-level comprehension of school-age children: A meta-analysis. *Journal of Research on Educational Effectiveness, 2,* 1–44.

Eller, G., Pappas, C. C., & Brown, E. (1988). The lexical development of kindergartners: Learning from written context. *Journal of Reading Behavior, 20,* 5–24.

Elster, C. H. (2005). *What's in the word?: Word play, word lore and answers to your peskiest questions about language.* Fort Washington, PA: Harvest Books.

Evans, K. (2002). Fifth-grade students' perceptions of how they experience literature discussion groups. *Reading Research Quarterly, 37*(1), 46–69.

Fang, Z., & Schleppegrell, M. J. (2010). Disciplinary literacies across content areas: Supporting secondary reading through functional language analysis. *Journal of Adolescent and Adult Literacy, 53,* 587–597.

Fang, Z., Schleppegrell, M. J., & Cox, B. E. (2006). Understanding the language demands of schooling: Nouns in academic registers. *Journal of Literacy Research, 38*(3), 247–273.

Farstrup, A. E., & Samuels, S. J. (Eds.). (2008). *What research has to say about vocabulary instruction.* Newark, DE: International Reading Association.

Fisher, D., & Frey, N. (2008). *Word wise and content rich: Five essential steps to teaching academic vocabulary*. Portsmouth, NH: Heinemann.

Fisher, D., & Frey, N. (2010). Unpacking the language purpose: Vocabulary, structure and function. *TESOL Journal, 1*(3), 315–337.

Fisher, P. J., Blachowicz, C. L. Z., & Smith, J. C. (1991). Vocabulary learning in literature discussion groups. In J. Zutell & S. McCormick (Eds.), *Learner factors/teacher factors: Issues in literacy research and instruction: Fortieth Yearbook of the National Reading Conference* (pp. 201–209). Chicago: National Reading Conference.

Fletcher, M., & Santoli, S. (2003). *Reading to learn concepts in mathematics: An action research project*. Mobile: University of South Alabama. (Retrieved from ERIC database ED482001)

Flood, J., Lapp, D., & Fisher, D. (2003). Reading comprehension instruction. In J. Flood, D. Lapp, J. R. Squire, & J. M. Jensen (Eds.), *Handbook of research on teaching the English language arts* (2nd ed., pp. 931–941. Mahwah, NJ: Erlbaum.

Francis, M. A., & Simpson, M. L. (2003). Using theory, our intuition, and a research study to enhance students' vocabulary knowledge. *Journal of Adolescent and Adult Literacy, 47*, 66–78.

Freire, P. (1972). *Pedagogy of the oppressed*. Harmondsworth, UK: Penguin.

Frey, N., & Fisher, D. (2009). *Learning words inside and out*. Portsmouth, NH: Heinemann.

Fukkink, R. G., & de Glopper, K. (1998). Effects of instruction in deriving word meaning from context: A meta-analysis. *Review of Educational Research, 68*, 450–469.

Funk, C. E. (2007). *Thereby hangs a tale: Stories of curious word origins*. New York: Collins.

Gallagher, K. (2011). *Write like this: Teaching real-world writing through modeling and mentor texts*. Portland, ME: Stenhouse.

Garcia, G. E. (1991). Factors influencing the English Reading Test performance of Spanish-speaking Hispanic children. *Reading Research Quarterly, 26*(4), 371–392.

Gay, A. S. (2008). Helping teachers connect vocabulary and conceptual understanding. *Mathematics Teacher, 102*(3), 218–223.

Gay, G. (2000). *Culturally responsive teaching: Theory, research, and practice*. New York: Teachers College Press.

Gee, J. P. (2010). *An introduction to discourse analysis: Theory and method* (3rd ed.). New York: Routledge.

Gersten, R., Dimino, J., Jayanthi, M., Kim, J. S., & Santoro, L. E. (2010). Teacher study group: Impact of the professional development model on reading instruction and student outcomes in first grade classrooms. *American Educational Research Journal, 47*(3), 694–739.

Gillespie, A., Graham, S., Kiuhara, S., & Hebert, M. (2014). High school teachers' use of writing to support students' learning: A national survey. *Reading and Writing, 27*, 1043–1072.

González, N., Moll, L., & Amanti, C. (2005). *Funds of knowledge: Theorizing practices in households, communities, and classrooms*. Mahwah, NJ: Erlbaum.

Goodwin, A. P., Gilbert, J. K., & Cho, S. (2013). Morphological contributions to adolescent word reading: An item response approach. *Reading Research Quarterly, 48*(1), 39–60.

Graham, J., & Hodgson, T. (2008). Speaking math using chat in the multicultural math classroom. *Learning and Leading with Technology, 35*(5), 24–27.

Grant, M. C., & Fisher, D. (2010). *Reading and writing in science*. Thousand Oaks, CA: Corwin.

Graves, M. F. (1986). Vocabulary learning and instruction. In E. Z. Rothkopf (Ed.), *Review of research in education* (Vol. 13, pp. 49–89). Washington, DC: American Educational Research Association.

Graves, M. F. (2004). Theories and constructs that have made a significant difference in adolescent literacy—but have the potential to produce still more positive benefits. In T. L. Jetton

& J. A. Dole (Eds), *Adolescent literacy research and practice* (pp. 433–452). New York: Guilford Press.

Graves, M. F. (2006). *The vocabulary book: Learning and instruction.* New York: Teachers College Press.

Graves, M. F. (Ed.). (2009). *Essential readings on vocabulary instruction.* Newark, DE: International Reading Association.

Graves, M. F., Baumann, J. F., Blachowicz, C. L. Z., Manyak, P., Bates, A., Cieply, C., et al. (2014). Words, words everywhere but which ones do we teach? *The Reading Teacher, 67*(5), 333–346.

Graves, M. F., & Watts Taffe, S. M. (2002). The place of word consciousness in a research-based vocabulary program. In A. E. Farstrup & S. J. Samuels (Eds.), *What research has to say about reading instruction* (3rd ed., pp. 140–165). Newark, DE: International Reading Association.

Haggard, M. R. (1982). The vocabulary self-collection strategy: An active approach to word learning. *Journal of Reading, 26,* 203–207.

Halliday, M., & Hasan, R. (1989). *Language, context, and text: Aspects of language in a social-semiotic perspective.* Oxford, UK: Oxford University Press.

Hart, B., & Risley, T. R. (1995). *Meaningful differences in the everyday experience of young American children.* Baltimore, MD: Brookes.

Herr, N. (2008). *The sourcebook for teaching science: Strategies, activities, and instructional resources.* San Francisco: Jossey-Bass.

Hiebert, E. H., & Cervetti, G. N. (2012). What differences in narrative and informational texts mean for the learning and instruction of vocabulary. In E. J. Kame'enui & J. F. Baumann (Eds.), *Vocabulary instruction: Research to practice* (2nd ed., pp. 322–334). New York: Guilford Press.

Hiebert, E. H., & Kamil, M. L. (Eds.). (2005). *Teaching and learning vocabulary: Bringing research to practice.* Mahwah, NJ: Erlbaum.

Hiebert, E. H., & Lubliner, S. (2008). The nature, learning, and instruction of general academic vocabulary. In A. E. Farstrup & S. J. Samuels (Eds.), *What research has to say about vocabulary instruction* (pp. 106–129). Newark, DE: International Reading Association.

Hole, G. (2005). *The real McCoy: Why we say the things we say.* New York: Oxford University Press.

Hyland, K., & Tse, P. (2007). Is there an "academic vocabulary"? *TESOL Quarterly, 41*(2), 235–253.

Jackson, J., Tripp, S., & Cox, K. (2011). Interactive word walls: Transforming content vocabulary instruction. *Science Scope, 35*(3), 45–49.

Janks, H. (2010). *Literacy and power.* New York: Routledge.

Jiminez, R. J. (1997). The strategic reading abilities and potential of five low-literacy Latina/o readers in middle school. *Reading Research Quarterly, 32,* 224–243.

Kame'enui, E. J., & Baumann, J. F. (Eds.). (2012). *Vocabulary instruction: Research to practice* (2nd ed.). New York: Guilford Press.

Khourey-Bowers, C. (2011). Active learning strategies: The top 10. *The Science Teacher, 78*(4), 38–42.

Kieffer, M., & Lesaux, N. (2007). Breaking down words to build meaning: Morphology, vocabulary, and reading comprehension in the urban classroom. *The Reading Teacher, 61,* 134–144.

Kim, J. S., & White, T. G. (2008). Scaffolding voluntary summer reading for children in grades 3 to 5: An experimental study. *Scientific Studies of Reading, 12,* 1–23.

Ladson-Billings, G. (1994). *The dreamkeepers: Successful teachers for African-American children.* San Francisco: Jossey-Bass.

Lederer, R. (1990). *Crazy English* New York: Simon & Schuster.

Lederer, R. (1991). *The miracle of language.* New York: Simon & Schuster.

Lee, C. (1993). *Signifying as a scaffold to literary interpretation: The pedagogical implication of a form of African-American discourse* (NCTE Research Report No. 26). Urbana, IL: National Council of Teachers of English.

Lee, O., Quinn, H., & Valdes, G. (2013). Science and language for English Language Learners in relation to Next Generation Science Standards and with implications for Common Core State Standards for English Language Arts and Mathematics. *Educational Researcher, 42,* 223–233.

Lesaux, N. K., Kieffer, M. J., Faller, S. E., & Kelley, J. G. (2010). The effectiveness and ease of implementation of an academic English vocabulary intervention for linguistically diverse students in urban middle schools. *Reading Research Quarterly, 45,* 196–228.

Lewin, T. (2014, March 6). A new SAT aims to realign with schoolwork. *New York Times,* p. A1.

Lubliner, S., & Scott, J. A. (2008). *Nourishing vocabulary: Balancing words and learning.* Thousand Oaks, CA: Corwin Press.

MacKinnon, J. W. (1993). *A comparison of three schema-based methods of vocabulary instruction.* Unpublished doctoral dissertation, Florida State University. Gainsville.

Manyak, P. (2007). Character trait vocabulary: A schoolwide approach. *The Reading Teacher, 60,* 574–577.

Marzano, R. J. (2004). *Building background knowledge for academic achievement.* Alexandria, VA: Association for Supervision and Curriculum Development.

Marzano, R. J., & Pickering, D. (2005). *Building academic vocabulary.* Alexandria, VA: Association for Supervision and Curriculum Development.

Mattera, D. (1998). Afrika Road. In C. Larson (Ed.), *Under African skies: Modern African short stories* (pp. 222–227). New York: Farrar, Straus & Giroux.

McCutcheon, D., Green, L., & Abbott, R. (2008). Children's morphological knowledge: Links to literacy. *Reading Psychology, 29*(4), 289–314.

McKeown, M. G., & Beck, I. L. (1988). Learning vocabulary: Different ways for different goals. *Remedial and Special Education, 9,* 42–45.

McKeown, M. G., & Beck, I. L. (2004). Direct and rich vocabulary instruction. In J. F. Baumann & E. J. Kame'enui (Eds.), *Vocabulary instruction* (pp. 13–27). New York: Guilford Press.

McKeown, M. G., Beck, I. L., Omanson, R. C., & Pople, M. T. (1985). Some effects of the nature and frequency of vocabulary instruction on the knowledge and use of words. *Reading Research Quarterly, 20,* 522–535.

McTighe, J., & Lyman, F. T. (1988) Cueing thinking in the classroom: The promise of theory-embedded tools. *Educational Leadership, 45*(7), 18–24.

McTigue, E., & Croix, A. (2010). Visual literacy in science. *Science Scope, 33*(9), 17–22.

Medina, T. N., Snedeker, J., Trueswell, J. C., & Gleitman, L R. (2011). How words can and cannot be learned by observation. *Proceedings of the National Academy of Sciences, 108,* 9014–9019.

Mezynski, K. (1983). Issues concerning the acquisition of knowledge: Effects of vocabulary training on reading comprehension. *Review of Educational Research, 53,* 253–279.

Milewski, B., Johnsen, D., Glazer, N., & Kubota. M. (2005). *A survey to evaluate the alignment of the new SAT writing and critical reading sections to curricula and instructional practices: College Board Research Report No. 2005-1, ETS RR-05-07.* New York: College Entrance Examination Board.

Miller, K. R., & Levine, J. (2006). *Biology.* Upper Saddle River, NJ: Pearson Prentice Hall.

Moore-Russo, D., & Shanahan, L. E. (2014). A broader vision of literacy: Including the visual with the linguistic. *Journal of Adolescent and Adult Literacy, 57*(7), 527–532.

Murray, M. (2004). *Teaching mathematics vocabulary in context.* Portsmouth, NH: Heinemann.

Nagy, W. E. (1988). *Teaching vocabulary to improve comprehension.* Newark, DE: International Reading Association.

Nagy, W. E. (2005). Why vocabulary instruction needs to be long-term and comprehensive. In E. H. Hiebert & M. L. Kamil (Eds.), *Teaching and learning vocabulary: Bringing research to practice* (pp. 27–44). Mahwah, NJ: Erlbaum.

Nagy, W. E., Anderson, R. C., & Herman, P. A. (1987). Learning word meanings from context during normal reading. *American Educational Research Journal, 24,* 237–270.

Nagy, W. E., & Herman, P. A. (1984). *Limitations of vocabulary instruction* (Tech. Report No. 326). Urbana: University of Illinois Center for the Study of Reading. (ERIC Document Reproduction Services No. ED248498)

Nagy, W. E., & Herman, P. A. (1987). Breadth and depth of vocabulary knowledge: Implications for acquisition and instruction. In M. G. McKeown & M. E. Curtis (Eds.), *The nature of vocabulary acquisition* (pp. 19–35). Hillsdale, NJ: Erlbaum.

Nagy, W. E., Herman, P. A., & Anderson, R. C. (1985). Learning words from context. *Reading Research Quarterly, 20,* 233–253.

Nagy, W. E., & Scott, J. A. (2000). Vocabulary processes. In M. L. Kamil, P. B. Mosenthal, P. D. Pearson, & R. Barr (Eds.), *Handbook of reading research* (Vol. 3, pp. 269–284). Mahwah, NJ: Erlbaum.

Nagy, W. E., & Townsend, D. (2012) Words as tools: Learning academic vocabulary as language acquisition. *Reading Research Quarterly, 47*(1), 91–108.

National Association of Secondary School Principals. (2013). *Breaking ranks.* Reston, VA: Author.

National Center for Educational Statistics. (2010). *U.S. history 2010: National assessment of educational progress at grades 4, 8, and 12.* Washington, DC: National Center for Educational Statistics, Institute of Educational Statistics, U.S. Department of Education.

National Governors Association & Council of Chief State School Officers. (2010a). *Common Core State Standards for English language arts and literacy in history/social studies, science, and technical subjects.* Washington, DC: Authors.

National Governors Association & Council of Chief State School Officers. (2010b). *Common Core State Standards for mathematics.* Washington, DC: Authors.

National Research Council. (2011). Next Generation Science Standards. Retrieved September 2014, from *www.nextgenscience.org.*

Neugebauer, S. R., & Currie-Rubin, R. (2009). Read-alouds in Calca, Peru: A bilingual indigenous context. *The Reading Teacher, 62*(5), 396–405.

Ogle, D. (2000) Make it visual: A picture is worth a thousand words. In M. McLaughlin & M. E. Vogt (Eds.), *Creativity and innovation in content area teaching* (pp. 55–71). Norwood, MA: Christopher Gordon.

Ogle, D. (2010). Comprehension in social studies. In K. Ganske & D. Fisher (Eds.), *Comprehension across the curriculum: Perspectives and practices* (pp. 160–174). New York: Guilford Press.

Ogle, D., & Correa-Kovtun, A. (2010). Supporting English language learners and struggling readers with the "Partner Reading and Content, Too" routine. *The Reading Teacher, 63*(7), 532–542.

Ogle, D., Klemp, R., & McBride, W. (2007). *Building literacy in social studies.* Alexandria, VA: Association for Supervision and Curriculum Development.

Ogle, D., & Lang, L. (2011). Best practices in adolescent literacy instruction. In L. M. Morrow & L. B. Gambrell (Eds.), *Best practices in literacy instruction* (4th ed., pp. 138–173). New York: Guilford Press.

Pany, D., Jenkins, J. R., & Schreck, J. (1982). Vocabulary instruction: Effects on word knowledge and reading comprehension. *Learning Disabilities Quarterly, 5,* 202–215.

Passig, D. (2003). A taxonomy of future higher thinking skills. *Informatics in Education, 2*, 79–92. Retrieved October 4, 2011, from *http://dl.acm.org/citation.cfm?id=937521.*

Pigada, M., & Schmitt, N. (2006). Vocabulary acquisition from extensive reading: A case study. *Reading in a Foreign Language, 18*(1), 1–28.

Pressley, M., & Allington, R. L. (2014). *Reading instruction that works: The case for balanced teaching* (4th ed.). New York: Guilford Press.

Pries, C. H., & Hughes, J. (2012). Inquiring into familiar objects: An inquiry-based approach to introduce scientific vocabulary. *Science Activities, 49*, 64–69.

Programme for International Student Assessment. (2012). *PISA 2009 technical report.* Paris: Organisation for Economic Co-operation and Development (OECD). Retrieved from *www.oecd.org/dataoecd/60/31/50036771.pdf.*

Phythian-Sence, R. E., & Wagner, R. K. (2007). Vocabulary acquisition: A primer. In R. K. Wagner, A. E. Muse, & K. R. Tanneanbaum (Eds.), *Vocabulary acquisition: Implications for reading comprehension* (pp. 1–14). New York: Guilford Press.

Rasinski, T. V., Padak, N., Newton, J., & Newton, E. (2011). The Latin–Greek connection: Building vocabulary through morphological study. *The Reading Teacher, 65*, 133–141.

Ray, K. W. (1999). *Wondrous words: Writers and writing in the elementary classroom.* Urbana, IL: National Council of Teachers of English.

Riddle Buly, M., & Valencia, S. W. (2002). Below the bar: Profiles of students who fail state reading tests. *Educational Evaluation and Policy Analysis, 24*, 219–239.

Roman, L., & Roman, M. (2010). *Encyclopedia of Greek and Roman mythology.* New York: Facts on File.

Ross, D., Fisher, D., & Frey, N. (2009). The art of argumentation. *Science and Children, 47*(3), 28–31.

Ruddell, M. R., & Shearer, B. A. (2002). "Extraordinary," "tremendous," "exhilarating," "magnificent": Middle school at-risk students become avid word learners with the vocabulary self-collection strategy (VSS). *Journal of Adolescent and Adult Literacy, 45*, 352–363.

Sadoski, M., Goetz, E. T., & Fritz, J. B. (1993). Impact of concreteness on comprehensibility, interest, and memory for text: Implications for dual coding theory and text design. *Journal of Educational Psychology, 85*, 291–304.

Sampson, V., Enderle, P., Grooms, J., & Witte, S. (2013). Writing to learn by learning to write during the high school science laboratory: Helping middle and high school students develop argumentative writing skills as they learn core ideas. *Science Education, 97*, 643–670.

Santa, C. M., Havens, L. T., & Valdes, B. J. (2004). *Project CRISS: Creating independence through student-owned strategies* (3rd ed.). Dubuque, IA: Kendall/Hunt.

Schleppegrell, M. J. (2004). *The language of schooling: A functional linguistic perspective.* Mahwah, NJ: Erlbaum.

Schultz, J. E., Hollowell, K. A., Ellis, W., Jr., & Kennedy, P. A. (2004). *Geometry.* Austin, TX: Holt, Rhinehart, & Winston.

Schwanenflugel, P. J., Stahl, S. A., & McFalls, E. L. (1997). *Partial word knowledge and vocabulary growth during reading comprehension* (Research Report No. 76). University of Georgia, National Reading Research Center.

Schwartz, R. M., & Raphael, T. E. (1985). Concept of definition: A key to improving students' vocabulary. *The Reading Teacher, 39*, 198–205.

Scott, J. A., Flinspach, S. L., & Vevea, J. L. (2011, May). *Identifying and teaching vocabulary in fourth- and fifth-grade math and science.* Paper presented at the 61st annual conference of the Literacy Research Association, Jacksonville, FL.

Scott, J. A., Jamieson-Noel, D., & Asselin, M. (2003). Vocabulary instruction throughout the day in twenty-three Canadian upper-elementary classrooms. *The Elementary School Journal, 103*, 269–286.

Scott, J. A., Miller, T. F., & Flinspach, S. L. (2012). Developing word consciousness: Lessons from highly diverse fourth-grade classrooms. In E. J. Kame'enui & J. F. Baumann (Eds.), *Vocabulary instruction: Research to practice* (2nd ed., pp. 169–188). New York: Guilford Press.

Scott, J. A., Nagy, W. E., & Flinspach, S. L. (2008). More than merely words: Redefining vocabulary learning in a culturally and linguistically diverse society. In A. E. Farstrup & S. J. Samuels (Eds.), *What research has to say about vocabulary instruction* (pp. 182–210). Newark, DE: International Reading Association.

Scott, J. A., Skobel, B. J., & Wells, J. (2008). *The word-conscious classroom: Building the vocabulary readers and writers need*. New York: Scholastic.

Serafini, F., & Giorgis, C. (2003). *13 reasons to read aloud with older students: Fostering the intellectual life with older readers*. Portsmouth, NH: Heinemann.

Seuss, Dr. [T. S. Geisel]. (1960). *Green eggs and ham*. New York: Random House.

Shanahan, T., & Shanahan, C. (2008). Teaching disciplinary literacy to adolescents: Rethinking content-area literacy. *Harvard Educational Review, 78*(1), 40–59.

Shook, A. C., Hazelcorn, M., & Lozano, E. R. (2011). Science vocabulary for all: Strategies to improve vocabulary in an inclusive biology class. *The Science Teacher, 78*(3), 45–49.

Slough, S. W., McTigue, E. M., Kim, S., & Jennings, S. K. (2010). Science textbooks use of graphical representations: A descriptive analysis of four sixth-grade science texts. *Reading Psychology, 31*(3), 301–325.

Smith, T. B. (2008). Teaching vocabulary expeditiously: Three keys to improving vocabulary instruction. *English Journal, 97*(4), 20–25.

Snow, C., Lawrence, J., & White, C. (2009). Generating knowledge of academic language among urban middle school students. *Journal of Research on Educational Effectiveness, 2*(4), 325–344.

Stahl, S. A. (2005). Four problems with teaching word meanings and what to do to make vocabulary an integral part of instruction. In E. H. Hiebert & M. J. Kamil (Eds.), *Teaching and learning vocabulary: Bringing research to practice* (pp. 95–115). Mahwah, NJ: Erlbaum.

Stahl, S. A., & Fairbanks, M. M. (1986). The effects of vocabulary instruction: A model-based meta-analysis. *Review of Educational Research, 56*, 72–110.

Stahl, S. A., & Nagy, W. E. (2006). *Teaching word meanings*. Mahwah, NJ: Erlbaum.

Swanborn, M. S. L., & de Glopper, K. (1999). Incidental word learning while reading: A meta-analysis. *Review of Educational Research, 69*, 261–285.

Templeton, S. (2012). The vocabulary–spelling connection and generative instruction: Morphological knowledge at the intermediate grades and beyond. In E. J. Kame'enui & J. F. Baumann (Eds.), *Vocabulary instruction: Research to practice* (pp. 116–138). New York: Guilford Press.

Tomeson, M., & Aarnoutse, C. (1998). Effects of an instructional programme for deriving word meanings. *Educational Studies, 24*, 107–128.

Townsend, D., Filippini, A., Collins, P., & Biancarosa, G. (2012). Evidence for the importance of academic word knowledge for the academic achievement of diverse middle school students. *Elementary School Journal, 113*, 497–519.

van Kleeck, A., Stahl, S., & Bauer, E. (Eds.). (2003). *On reading books to children: Parents and teachers*. Mahwah, NJ: Erlbaum.

Vosniadou, S., & Ortony, A. (1983). The emergence of the literal–metaphorical–anomalous distinction in young children. *Child Development, 54*, 154–161.

Watkins, P. A., & Leto, G. K. (1994). *Life science*. Austin, TX: Holt, Rinehart & Winston.

Watts Taffe, S., Blachowicz, C. L. Z., & Fisher. P. J. (2009). Vocabulary instruction for diverse students. In L. M. Morrow, R. Rueda, & D. Lapp (Eds.), *Handbook of research on literacy and diversity* (pp. 320–336). New York: Guilford Press.

Welty, E. (1982). Circe. In *The Collected Stories of Eudora Welty*. New York: Houghton Mifflin Harcourt.

Wheeler, D. (2014). Do students still have free speech in schools? Retrieved August 11, 2014, from *www.theatlantic.com/education/archive/2014/04/do-students-still-have-free-speech-in-school/360266*.

White, T. G., Graves, M. F., & Slater, W. H. (1990). Growth of reading vocabulary in diverse elementary schools: Decoding and word meaning. *Journal of Educational Psychology, 82*, 281–290.

Whittlesea, B. W. (1987). Preservation of specific experiences in the representation of general knowledge. *Journal of Experimental Psychology: Learning, Memory, and Cognition, 13*(1), 3–17.

Winchester, S. (2005). *The professor and the madman*. New York: Harper Perennial.

Wray, D. (2001, July 12–14). *Developing factual writing: An approach through scaffolding*. Paper presented at the European Reading Conference, Dublin, Ireland.

Zichermann, G., & Cunningham, C. (2011). *Gamification by design: Implementing game mechanics in web and mobile apps*. New York: O'Reilly Media.

Zusak, M. *The book thief*. New York: Knopf.

Zwiers, J. (2008). *Building academic language: Essential practices in content classrooms*. San Francisco: Jossey-Bass.

Zwiers, J., & Crawford, M. (2011). *Academic conversation: Classroom talk that fosters critical thinking and content understandings*. Portland, ME: Stenhouse.

Index

Note. f or *t* following a page number indicates a figure or a table.